TROU[...]

Keeping The Alli[...]

LYMAN COLEMAN

Managing Editor
DENISE BELTZNER

Assistant Editors
DOUGLAS LABUDDE
KEITH MADSEN
STEPHEN SHEELY

Cover Art
CHRISTOPHER WERNER

Cover Design
ERIKA TIEPEL

Layout Production
FRONTLINE GROUP
SHARON PENINGTON

Seven Strategies for Draining the Swamp

SESSION	ENTRY LEVEL	ADVANCED LEVEL
1 ORIENTATION	Learning to Cope: Isaiah 40:25–31	
2 WHEN WORRY HITS	Worry Warts: Matthew 6:25–34	Victory Over Worry: Philippians 4:2–9
3 WHEN YOU ARE HURT	Forgive and Forget: Matthew 18:21–35	Loving Relationships: Romans 12:9–21
4 WHEN STRESS BUILDS	Too Busy: Luke 10:38–42	Overcoming Overload: 2 Corinthians 1:3–11
5 WHEN YOU FAIL	Down, But Not Out: Luke 22:54–62	God's Grace For All: 1 Timothy 1:12–20
6 WHEN TRAGEDY STRIKES	Going Home: John 14:1–6	Perseverance: 2 Corinthians 4:8–18
7 WHEN QUESTIONS REMAIN	Renewal of Hope: Luke 24:13–32	Eternal Hope: Romans 8:18–25,31–39

Serendipity House / Box 1012 / Littleton, CO 80160
1-800-525-9563 / www.serendipityhouse.com
© 1995 Serendipity House. All Rights Reserved
97 98 99 / **201F series•CHG** / 4 3

ACKNOWLEDGMENTS

To Zondervan Bible Publishers
for permission to use
the NIV text,
The Holy Bible, New International Bible Society.
© 1973, 1978, 1984 by International Bible Society.
Used by permission of Zondervan Bible Publishers

Instructions for Group Leader

PURPOSE: **What is this course all about?** This course allows you to deal with troubles in your life in a supportive group relationship.

SEEKERS/ STRUGGLERS: **Who is this course designed for?** Two kinds of people: (a) Seekers who do not know where they are with God but are open to finding out, and (b) Strugglers who are committed to Jesus Christ, but want to grow in their faith.

NEW PEOPLE: **Does this mean I can invite my non-church friends?** Absolutely. In fact, this would be a good place for people on their way back to God to start.

STUDY: **What are we going to study?** Seven common troubles in our lives (see Table of Contents) and Biblical strategies for dealing with them.

FIRST SESSION: **What do we do at the meetings?** In the first session, you get acquainted and decide on the Ground Rules for your group. In sessions two through seven, you have two options for Bible study.

TWO OPTIONS: **What are the two options?** OPTION 1—This study is best for newly-formed groups or groups that are unfamiliar with small group Bible study. This option primarily contains multiple-choice questions, with no "right or wrong" answers.

OPTION 2—This study is best for groups who have had previous small group Bible studies and want to dig deeper into the Scriptures. Option 2 questions are deeper—and the Scripture is a teaching passage.

CHOOSING AN OPTION: **Which option of Bible study do you recommend?** The OPTION 1 study is best for newly-formed groups, groups that are unfamiliar with small group Bible study, or groups that are only meeting for an hour. The OPTION 2 study is best for deeper Bible study groups, or groups which meet for more than an hour.

CHOOSING BOTH OPTIONS:	**Can we choose both options?** If your group meets for 90–120 minutes, you can choose to do both studies at the same time. Or you can spend two weeks on a unit—OPTION 1 the first week and OPTION 2 the next. Or you can do one of the options in the meeting and the other option for homework.
SMALL GROUP:	**What's different about this course?** It is written for a small group to do together.
GROUP BUILDING:	**What is the purpose behind your approach to Bible study?** To give everyone a chance to share their own "spiritual story," and to bond as a group. This is often referred to as "koinonia."
KOINONIA:	**What is koinonia and why is it a part of these studies?** Koinonia means "fellowship." It is an important part of these sessions, because as a group gets to know one another, they are more willing to share their needs and care for one another.
BIBLE KNOWLEDGE:	**What if I don't know much about the Bible?** No problem. Option 1 is based on a Bible story that stands on its own—to discuss as though you were hearing it for the first time. Both options come with occasional Comments—to keep you up to speed.
COMMENTS:	**What is the purpose of the Comments in the studies?** To help you understand the context of the Bible passage.
LEADERSHIP:	**Who leads the meetings?** Ideally, there should be three people: (a) trained leader, (b) apprentice or co-leader, and (c) host. Having an apprentice-in-training in the group, you have a built-in system for multi-plying the group if it gets too large. In fact, this is one of the goals of the group—to give "birth" to a new group in time.

Beginning a Small Group

1. AGENDA: There are three parts to every group meeting.

GATHERING	BIBLE STUDY	CARING TIME
15 min.	30 min.	15–45 min.
Purpose:	Purpose:	Purpose:
To break the ice	To share your spiritual journey	To share prayer requests

2. FEARLESS FOURSOME: If you have more than seven in your group at any time, call the option play when the time comes for Bible study, and sub-divide into groups of 4 for greater participation. (In 4s, everyone will share and you can finish the Bible study in 30 minutes.) Then regather the group for the CARING TIME.

GATHERING	BIBLE STUDY	CARING TIME
All Together	Groups of 4	Back Together

3. EMPTY CHAIR: Pull up an empty chair during the CARING TIME at the close and ask God to fill this chair each week. Remember, by breaking into groups of 4 for the Bible study time, you can grow numerically without feeling "too big" as a group.

The Group Leader needs an apprentice-in-training at all times so that the apprentice can start a new "cell" when the group size is 12 or more.

SESSION 1
Orientation

PURPOSE

To get acquainted, to share your expectations, and to decide on the ground rules for your group.

AGENDA

 Gathering   Bible Study   Caring Time

OPEN

GATHERING / 15 Minutes / All Together

Leader: The purpose of the Gathering time is to break the ice. Read the instructions for Step One and go first. Then read the Introduction (Step Two) and the instructions for the Bible Study.

Step One: How'd It Go Today? What kind of day did you have today? Introduce yourself to the group by marking an "**✗**" on the lines below, which best describes the kind of day you've had today. Then go around the group and explain why you marked what you did. If there are people in the group who do not know each other, start by introducing yourselves to each other. (This ice-breaker, and many more like it, can be found in Serendipity's book *Ice-Breakers and Heart-Warmers*.)

Barefoot in the Park _____Nightmare on Elm Street

Sunny ___✔_____Stormy

I felt like a princess_____I felt like a gym shoe

Ants _____✔___Grasshopper

Miss America _____Bad hair day

Wonder Dog_____Fire Hydrant

Baseball _____Louisville Slugger

Tasmanian Devil _____Rip Van Winkle

King Midas _____Court Jester

Mother Teresa _____Madonna

Statue _____Pigeon

Step Two: Welcome. Welcome to this small group study on troubles. There isn't a person alive who sails through life without experiencing troubles. Some have more troubles than others, but we all face rough times. As Job's friend Eliphaz put it, "man is born to trouble as surely as sparks fly upward" (Job 5:7). These troubles may be anything from a series of overdrafts at the bank to disciplinary problems with your kids to full-fledged crises like divorce or bankruptcy. The only thing certain is that troubles come. That is the *bad* news.

The *good* news is we don't have to let these troubles defeat us. First, we need to accept that times of trouble come to everyone. Then we can utilize the resources that are available to us through the strength of God, the support of friends and guidance from the Bible. Finally, we can flow past these troubles like an experienced river guide over white water. When we make it to the other side, we will feel relief and exhilaration.

In our time together, we will study the common troubles of life. These common troubles include worry, hurt, stress, failure and tragedy. We will end our time together looking at the ageless question, "Why me, Lord?"

THREE PARTS TO A SESSION

Every session has three parts: (1) **Gathering**—to break the ice and introduce the topic, (2) **Bible Study**—to share your own study through a passage of Scripture, and (3) **Caring Time**—to decide what action you need to take in this area of your life and to support one another in this action.

In this course, the Bible Study approach is a little unique with a different focus. Usually, the content of the passage is the focus of the Bible Study. In this course, the focus will be on telling your "story," using the passage as a springboard.

BIBLE STUDY / 30 Minutes / Groups of 4

Leader: If you have more than 7 in this session, we recommend groups of 4—4 to sit around the dining table, 4 around the kitchen table, and 4 around a folding table. Ask one person in each foursome to be the Leader and to complete the Bible Study in the time allotted. Then regather for the Caring Time, allowing 15–45 minutes.

The following passage is from the writings of the prophet Isaiah. In chapters 1–35, Isaiah prophesied about the Assyrian threat against Judah and Jerusalem. In chapters 36–39, Isaiah spoke of Assyria's failure and warned about the future rise of Babylon and the exile of God's people to Babylon. In chapters 40–66, he wrote as though the exile were almost over. Read Isaiah 40:25–31 and share your answers to the questions which follow with your group. In each foursome, ask someone to be the Leader. Go around on the first question. Then go around on the next question, working through the questionnaire. After 30 minutes, the leader will call time and ask you to regather for the Caring Time.

^{25}"To whom will you compare me?
            Or who is my equal?" says the Holy One.
^{26}Lift your eyes and look to the heavens:
            Who created all these?
        He who brings out the starry host one by one,
            and calls them each by name.
        Because of his great power and mighty strength,
            not one of them is missing.
^{27}Why do you say, O Jacob,
            and complain, O Israel,
        "My way is hidden from the Lord;
            my cause is disregarded by my God"?
^{28}Do you not know?
            Have you not heard?
        The Lord is the everlasting God,
            the Creator of the ends of the earth.
        He will not grow tired or weary,
            and his understanding no one can fathom.
^{29}He gives strength to the weary,
            and increases the power of the weak.
^{30}Even youths grow tired and weary,
            and young men stumble and fall;
^{31}but those who hope in the Lord
            will renew their strength.
        They will soar on wings like eagles;
            they will run and not grow weary,
            they will walk and not be faint.

Isaiah 40:25–31, NIV

1. What picture would you draw to go along with this passage?
   - ❏ a lone contemplative figure beneath a starry sky
   - ❏ a field of marathon runners, with one runner stumbling
   - ❏ an eagle soaring up toward a mountain peak
   - ❏ a triumphant runner crossing the finish line
   - ❏ a weightlifter lifting a huge barbell over his head

2. As an adolescent, what usually caused you to "stumble and fall"?
   - ❏ my two left feet—I was a klutz.
   - ❏ peer pressure—I wanted to be liked.
   - ❏ my own curiosity to experience new things
   - ❏ my social awkwardness
   - ❏ my poor self-image
   - ❏ my impulsiveness
   - ❏ I seldom stumbled.

3. As an adolescent, who would you have described as the "wind beneath your wings"? (This is the person who helped you soar when you were feeling low.)
   - ☑ my mother
   - ☑ a grandparent
   - ☐ my best friend
   - ☐ an adult friend
   - ☐ my father
   - ☐ a special teacher
   - ☐ a pastor
   - ☐ nobody

4. This poetic message was given to people in exile. When have you felt most like an "exile," like a person who didn't belong?
   - ☐ in junior high
   - ☐ when I moved to a new community as a child or adolescent
   - ☐ when I moved to a new community as an adult
   - ☐ when I went to college away from home
   - ☐ when I took a job that didn't fit me
   - ☐ when I was in a group where I was in the racial, cultural or religious minority
   - ☐ right now
   - ☐ I always feel like that.
   - ☐ I have never felt like that.
   - ☐ other: _____

5. What must we "exiles" understand before we are returned to our homeland (v. 28)?
   - ☑ that God calls the shots, not us
   - ☑ that God is ultimately in control
   - ☐ that God will not get tired and fall asleep on the job
   - ☐ that God helps those who help themselves
   - ☑ that God will take care of us in his time

6. As a weary exile, which of the following promises is the most uplifting and comforting?
   - ☐ "The Lord is the everlasting God" (v. 28).
   - ☐ "(The Lord is) the Creator of the ends of the earth" (v. 28).
   - ☐ "He will not grow tired or weary" (v. 28).
   - ☐ "and his understanding no one can fathom" (v. 28).
   - ☐ "He gives strength to the weary" (v. 29).
   - ☐ "and (he) increases the power of the weak" (v. 29).
   - ☐ "but those who hope in the Lord will renew their strength" (v. 31).
   - ☐ "They will soar on wings like eagles" (v. 31).
   - ☐ "they will run and not grow weary" (v. 31).
   - ☐ "they will walk and not be faint" (v. 31).

7. If you compared your present life to an eagle, where would you be?
   - ❏ soaring high—carried along by the wind
   - ☒ feeling a little turbulence—but I'm making it
   - ❏ tuckered out—it's been a long flight
   - ☒ wounded—but only buckshot wounds
   - ❏ other: _____

8. In which area of your life do you feel "faint"? _weakness_
   - ❏ in my personal life
   - ☒ in my family life
   - ❏ in my work/professional life
   - ❏ in my spiritual life
   - ❏ in my emotional life
   - ❏ other: _____

9. Describe the kind of strength you need from God right now:
   - ☒ to "soar like an eagle"—I want to do more than just survive and get by.
   - ❏ to "run and not grow weary"—I need to keep up the pace of my hectic life.
   - ❏ to "walk and not be faint"—I need help just to keep putting one foot in front of the other.
   - ❏ other: _____

10. What can this group do to help you find the strength you need?
    - ❏ simply listen to me as I share my troubles
    - ☒ keep pointing me to the strength I can find in God
    - ❏ just be there to walk with me
    - ☒ lift me up in prayer
    - ❏ share what has worked for them when facing similar troubles
    - ❏ other: _____

 CARING TIME / 15–45 Minutes / All Together

Leader: In this first session, take some time to discuss your expectations and to decide on the ground rules for your group. Then spend the remaining time in caring support for each other through sharing and prayer.

1. What motivated you to come to this group?
   - ❏ curiosity
   - ❏ A friend asked me.
   - ❏ I had nothing better to do.
   - ❏ a nagging suspicion that I'd better get my life together

"Never attempt to bear more than one kind of trouble at once. Some people bear all three kinds—all they have had, all they have now, and all they expect to have."
—Edward Everett Hale

EXPECTATIONS

2. As you begin this group, what are some goals or expectations you have for this course? Choose two or three of the following expectations and add one of your own:

    ❐ to discover ways to drain the "swamps of troubles" in my life
    ❐ to get to know some people who are willing to be open and honest about their troubles
    ❐ to relax and have fun—and forget about my troubles
    ❐ to see what the Bible says about my troubles and how to deal with them
    ❐ to deal with some of the issues in my life that create my troubles
    ❐ to gain a better understanding of God's love and care for me
    ❐ to see if God is saying anything to me about my life and his will for my life
    ❐ to gain some perspective on my troubles, so I don't feel so overwhelmed
    ❐ to allow Scripture to strengthen my faith to conquer these troubles with God's help
    ❐ other: _____

GROUND RULES

3. If you are going to commit the next six weeks or sessions to this group, what are some things you want understood by the group before you commit? Check two or three, and add any of your own:

    ❐ ATTENDANCE: To take the group seriously, and give the meetings priority.

    ❐ QUESTIONS ENCOURAGED: This is a support group for people who are struggling with all sorts of questions, including questions about their spiritual faith. Honest questions are encouraged.

    ❐ MISSION: This group will be "open" to anyone who is struggling, and also to anyone who is seeking or who is starting over in the Christian life ... and it will be the mission of this group to invite new people to the sessions.

    ❐ ACCOUNTABILITY: This group will be a support group. Prayer requests will be shared at the end of each session and group members are encouraged to call each other to ask, "How's it going?"

    ❐ CONFIDENTIALITY: Anything that is said in the group is kept in confidence.

    ❐ COVENANT: At the end of this course, the group will evaluate the experience and decide if they wish to continue as a covenant group.

SHARING | Take a few minutes to share prayer requests with other group members. Go around and answer this question first:

"How can we help you in prayer this week?"

PRAYER | Take a moment to pray together. If you have not prayed out loud before, finish the sentence:

"Hello, God, this is ... (first name). I want to thank you for ..."

ACTION | 1. Write down these verses of Scripture on a 3" x 5" card and place it somewhere where you will see it this week:

He gives strength to the weary ... but those who hope in the Lord will renew their strength. They will soar on wings like eagles; they will run and not grow weary, they will walk and not be faint.
Isaiah 40:29–31

2. Decide on where you are going to meet.

3. Ask someone to bring refreshments next week.

4. Encourage the group to invite a friend to the group next week—to fill the "empty chair" (see page 5).

SESSION 2
When Worry Hits

PURPOSE To develop strategies for dealing with worry.

AGENDA

 Gathering   Bible Study   Caring Time

OPEN

 ## GATHERING / 15 Minutes / All Together

Leader: The purpose of the Gathering time in this session is to help people get to know each other a bit better and share something personal about themselves. We encourage you to be the first one to share with the group by starting with Step One below. Then read Step Two (Introduction) and move on to the Bible Study.

Step One: Snapshots. Let the group take a look at some interesting scenes from your past. Choose two of the following "snapshots" of your life and tell your group about them.

- ❐ a time when I was really happy
- ❐ a time I toughed it out and accomplished my goal
- ❐ a time I took a big chance but it paid off
- ❐ a time I was really embarrassed
- ❐ a time I really chickened out
- ❐ a time I was really sad
- ❐ a time when I got into a bit of trouble

INTRODUCTION

Step Two: When Worry Hits. In this session, we will examine the trouble of worry. We live in a world that gives us many reasons to worry: economic woes, educational problems, rising crime rates, environmental concerns—to name a few! Often these global worries give us a sense of being out of control. After all, what can one person do about the national debt or the rate of increased violence?

But there are other worries as well. There are personal worries: "What type of future will my children have?" "How can I stretch my paycheck five more days?" "How can I possibly do everything I'm supposed to do and remain sane?" "Where can I find a reliable auto mechanic at a reasonable price?"

LEADER:
Choose the
OPTION 1 Bible
Study (below)
or the OPTION 2
Study (page 17).

However, if we spend all of our time and energy worrying about these things, we won't be able to enjoy the life God has given us. Contrary to what we think, worry is not a prerequisite for our lives. We can live a life that is not filled with worry.

In this session, you will have a chance to deal with the trouble of worry in your life. There are two options for the Bible Study. Option 1—for beginner groups—starts with a familiar passage from the Sermon on the Mount about worry. Option 2—for deeper groups—starts with Paul's letter to the Philippians, written in prison, with his words of encouragement for their times of trouble and difficulty.

 # BIBLE STUDY / 30 Minutes / Groups of 4

Leader: If you have more than 7 in this session, we recommend groups of 4—but not the same foursomes as last week. Ask one person in each foursome to be the Leader and complete the Bible Study in the time allotted. Remember, you have two choices for Bible Study: Option 1 and Option 2. Then regather for the Caring Time, allowing 15–45 minutes.

OPTION 1

Gospel Study / Worry Warts
Matthew 6:25–34

STUDY

Read Matthew 6:25–34 and discuss your responses to the following questions with your group. This passage is taken from the Sermon on the Mount, which Jesus shared with his followers.

> [25]*"Therefore I tell you, do not worry about your life, what you will eat or drink; or about your body, what you will wear. Is not life more important than food, and the body more important than clothes?* [26]*Look at the birds of the air; they do not sow or reap or store away in barns, and yet your heavenly Father feeds them. Are you not much more valuable than they?* [27]*Who of you by worrying can add a single hour to his life?*
>
> [28]*"And why do you worry about clothes? See how the lilies of the field grow. They do not labor or spin.* [29]*Yet I tell you that not even Solomon in all his splendor was dressed like one of these.* [30]*If that is how God clothes the grass of the field, which is here today and tomorrow is thrown into the fire, will he not much more clothe you, O you of little faith?* [31]*So do not worry, saying, 'What shall we eat?' or 'What shall we drink?' or 'What shall we wear?'* [32]*For the pagans run after all these things, and your heavenly Father knows that you need them.* [33]*But seek first his kingdom and his righteous-*

ness, and all these things will be given to you as well. [34]Therefore do not worry about tomorrow, for tomorrow will worry about itself. Each day has enough trouble of its own.

Matthew 6:25–34, NIV

1. Imagine that you are hearing this passage for the first time (and you did not know that Jesus said it). What would be your first reaction?
    - ❐ Sounds like a hippy from the '60s.
    - ❐ This person doesn't have a clue about the real world.
    - ❐ This person must be independently wealthy.
    - ❐ I wish it was that easy.
    - ❐ This is the kind of message our modern world needs.

2. When Jesus said, "Do not worry about your life," he meant:
    - ❐ Live one day at a time.
    - ❐ Don't plan for tomorrow.
    - ❐ Trusting God is a key part of planning for tomorrow.
    - ❐ Sit back and let God take care of you.
    - ❐ Worry is a waste of time and energy.

3. What things do you remember worrying about most in sixth grade?
    - ❐ forgetting my lunch money
    - ❐ what kind of mood the school bully was in
    - ❐ going to junior high and having to undress for gym class
    - ❐ whether a certain girl/boy liked me
    - ❐ if my friends realized I was starting to like the opposite sex
    - ❐ if the teacher would ask me for the homework I hadn't done
    - ❐ other: _____

4. Which two of the following situations are most worrisome to you?
    - ❐ whether I will ever marry
    - ❐ whether we can stay married
    - ❐ the safety of our children
    - ❐ gaining ten pounds
    - ❐ business in financial trouble
    - ❐ out-of-town relatives visiting
    - ❐ my job and how secure it is
    - ❐ spending the weekend alone
    - ❐ my favorite television show is preempted
    - ❐ bills and having enough money to pay them
    - ❐ whether our children will ever "amount to anything"
    - ❐ the economy and the fluctuations in the stock market
    - ❐ the instability of governments around the world
    - ❐ my child having problems at school
    - ❐ my health and being able to maintain good health

"Worry does not empty tomorrow of its sorrow; it empties today of its strength."
—Corrie ten Boom

5. Check the two areas of your life which concerned you the most 10 years ago, 5 years ago and last week. Do you find any similar concerns from year to year, week to week? What does that tell you?

category	10 years ago	5 years ago	last week
job	❏	❏	❏
sex	❏	❏	❏
money	❏	❏	❏
marriage	❏	❏	❏
parents	❏	❏	❏
politics	❏	❏	❏
health	❏	❏	❏
relationships	❏	❏	❏
children	❏	❏	❏
spiritual life	❏	❏	❏
retirement	❏	❏	❏

"It is distrust of God to be troubled about what is to come; impatience against God to be troubled with what is present; and anger at God to be troubled for what is past."
—Simon Patrick

6. How do you usually handle worry?
   ❏ What, me worry?
   ❏ I talk about it so much that others worry.
   ❏ I stay busy so I don't think about it.
   ❏ I let go and let God take care of it.
   ❏ I worry so much it worries me.
   ❏ I indulge in one of my vices to relieve the pressure.
   ❏ I seek professional help.

7. If you chose to live a simple life (like the Amish), what would change about your current circumstances?

8. If you could change one thing that causes you to worry, what would it be?
   ❏ overspending
   ❏ my job
   ❏ my priorities in life
   ❏ my health concerns
   ❏ expectations that I put on myself and others
   ❏ other: _____

LEADER: When you have completed the Bible Study, move on to the Caring Time (page 20).

9. Which of the actions suggested by this Scripture do you think would be your best next step in conquering worry?
   ❏ get back in touch with what is important in life (v. 25)
   ❏ get out into nature more to "look at the birds" and "consider the lilies" (vv. 26, 28)
   ❏ trust God for what I need (v. 32)
   ❏ seek first God's kingdom (v. 33)
   ❏ other: _____

Epistle Study / Victory Over Worry
Philippians 4:2–9

STUDY

Read Philippians 4:2–9 and share your responses to the following questions with your group. This is part of a message the apostle Paul wrote to his followers in Philippi from jail in Rome. Therefore, when Paul tells us to rejoice in the midst of troubles, he was not just writing "from an ivory tower."

²I plead with Euodia and I plead with Syntyche to agree with each other in the Lord. ³Yes, and I ask you, loyal yokefellow, help these women who have contended at my side in the cause of the gospel, along with Clement and the rest of my fellow workers, whose names are in the book of life.

⁴Rejoice in the Lord always. I will say it again: Rejoice! ⁵Let your gentleness be evident to all. The Lord is near. ⁶Do not be anxious about anything, but in everything, by prayer and petition, with thanksgiving, present your requests to God. ⁷And the peace of God, which transcends all understanding, will guard your hearts and your minds in Christ Jesus.

⁸Finally, brothers, whatever is true, whatever is noble, whatever is right, whatever is pure, whatever is lovely, whatever is admirable—if anything is excellent or praiseworthy—think about such things. ⁹Whatever you have learned or received or heard from me, or seen in me—put it into practice. And the God of peace will be with you.

Philippians 4:2–9, NIV

1. What in this passage surprises you?
   - ❐ that women were leaders in the early church (vv. 2–3)
   - ❐ that people fought in the early church just like they do today (v. 2)
   - ❐ that Paul could write of rejoicing and not being anxious while he was in jail (vv. 4, 6)
   - ❐ that Paul would so boldly present himself as an example (v. 9)

2. In your opinion, what is the most important thing Paul says about worry in this passage?
   - ❐ Rejoicing in the positive keeps us from focusing on and worrying about the negative.
   - ❐ Trusting our needs to God in prayer keeps us from worrying about them.
   - ❐ True peace comes from Jesus Christ.
   - ❐ Obedience to the teachings of God brings peace to our souls.

3. When Paul says, "Rejoice in the Lord always," he means:
   - ☐ We should shout "Praise God!" when we slam our finger in the car door.
   - ☐ We should rejoice that God brings hard times to our life.
   - ☐ We should find something to rejoice in, no matter what our circumstances.
   - ☐ We should not let circumstances keep us from celebrating the fact that God loves us.
   - ☐ other: _____

4. When in your life have you experienced something that seemed unfortunate at the time, but later you found something to rejoice in?

5. On a scale of 1 to 5 (1 = no worry and 5 = lots of worry), indicate how much worry each of the following events would cause you:

Loss of your job	1	2	3	4	5
Spouse's infidelity	1	2	3	4	5
Your serious illness	1	2	3	4	5
Conflict with best friend	1	2	3	4	5
Alienation from God	1	2	3	4	5
Loss of all your savings	1	2	3	4	5
Your child addicted to drugs or alcohol	1	2	3	4	5
Breakup with boy/girlfriend	1	2	3	4	5

6. Paul gives the following four commands to the church for dealing with problems in general. Which command would be most helpful to you right now?
   - ☐ "Rejoice in the Lord always" (v. 4).
   - ☐ "Let your gentleness be evident to all" (v. 5).
   - ☐ "Do not be anxious about anything" (v. 6).
   - ☐ "But in everything, by prayer and petition, with thanksgiving, present your requests to God" (v. 6).

7. In verse 8 Paul lists several virtues, perhaps drawn from the teaching of the philosophers of his day. The Philippians are to practice the kind of morality and behavior that would be commended even by the pagans. Rate yourself on a scale of 1 to 5 (1 = "I really need help with this" and 5 = "I'm doing rather well with this"):

___ TRUE: sincerity and accuracy in thought, word and deed
___ NOBLE: these qualities command respect and lift up one's mind from the mundane
___ RIGHT: literally, "just and fair"
___ PURE: a character unblemished by ulterior motives
___ LOVELY: the quality which calls forth love from others
___ ADMIRABLE: what people think only good things about
___ EXCELLENT: refers to moral excellence
___ PRAISEWORTHY: refers to behavior that is universally praised

LEADER: When you have completed the Bible Study, move on to the Caring Time (page 20).

8. How would you describe the degree of peace in your soul at this stage of your life?
   ❐ a peace that transcends all understanding
   ❐ a peace like a quiet, deep river
   ❐ well, maybe like a raging river with white water
   ❐ would you believe, a flooding river that's breaking through the dikes and there are more clouds on the horizon
   ❐ With me, it's just a dried-up river bed.

COMMENT

Paul pinpoints a specific problem confronting the Philippian church—Euodia and Syntyche have had a falling out. Their disunity is threatening the unity of the whole church. (It's easy to imagine individuals lining up behind one or the other of these women so that factions develop.) Paul first identifies the source of the disunity and then urges a resolution of the problem. But he does not stop at that point. He launches into a series of admonitions, which (if followed) will enable them to "agree with each other in the Lord" (v. 1). He identifies attitudes which help people to cope successfully in difficult times. In the process, Paul gives us a profound lesson about the mental state which promotes vital living.

Our basic attitude ought to be one of rejoicing rather than worrying. We can rejoice, not because we are blind to difficulties or because God will somehow magically take our problems away. We can rejoice because we know that we can offer all our anxieties to God in prayer. The implication is that God will hear and answer our prayers. In other words, God is in control—not our circumstances. No matter how bleak it might be (and both Paul and the Philippians were in tough situations), God is in control and he cares about us.

CARING TIME / 15–45 Minutes / All Together

Leader: The purpose of the Caring Time in this session is to spend time in caring support for each other through Sharing, Prayer, and Action.

SHARING

Take some time to share any personal prayer requests by answering this question:

"Where in your life do you need to relax and not worry so much this week, and how are you going to do it?"

PRAYER

Close with a short time of prayer, remembering the requests that were shared. Go around in a circle and give everyone an opportunity to pray. If you choose to pray in silence, say the word "Amen" when you finish your prayer, so that the next person will know when to start.

ACTION

1. Write down this Bible verse on a 3" x 5" card and place it somewhere where you will see it this week:

   Do not be anxious about anything, but in everything, by prayer and petition, with thanksgiving, present your requests to God. And the peace of God, which transcends all understanding, will guard your hearts and minds in Christ Jesus.

   Philippians 4:6–7

2. On an index card, write your first name and one prayer request you have about your relationship with God. Randomly distribute the cards, and ask each person to be in prayer for another group member throughout the next week.

SESSION 3
When You Are Hurt

PURPOSE   To learn ways to recover from being hurt in a relationship.

AGENDA

 **Gathering**    **Bible Study**   **Caring Time**

OPEN

 ## GATHERING / 15 Minutes / All Together

Leader: Read the instructions for Step One and set the pace by going first. Then read the Introduction in Step Two and move on to the Bible Study.

Step One: Power People. Some people are more than just people. There are people in your life who have a powerful effect on you. The different types of "power people" are listed below. In the blanks, list the family and friends who are the "power people" in your life:

_____LISTENER: The person who is always there to hear what I have to say without trying to change me.

_____CHALLENGER: That special person who has a way of bringing out the best in me, even when I'm complacent.

_____DEVIL'S ADVOCATE: One of those people who love me enough to tell me things I might not want to hear.

_____ENCOURAGER: Someone who has a way of helping me to look on the bright side of things.

_____PRAYER PARTNER: Someone I trust enough to come with me when I go to God in prayer.

_____ROLE MODEL: The kind of person I want to emulate in my actions, character, and reputation.

_____MENTOR: One of those people who is willing to take me under their wing and guide me on my life's journey.

_____INSPIRER: Someone who can elevate my spirit and remind me that God has everything in control.

_____CONSOLER: The person who can calm me down when life spins out of control.

_____PLAYMATE: Someone who I can always count on to do something fun and bring out the child in me.

_____DREAM PARTNER: That special person who will listen to and appreciate my dreams.

INTRODUCTION

Step Two: When You Are Hurt. Barbra Streisand sang, "People who need people, are the luckiest people in the world." We know that we need people in our lives. They provide us with a sense of companionship and connectedness to the world around us. Without relationships, life would not only be uninteresting, it would also be dehumanizing. Through our relationships, we learn what it means to be a created human being. The sociologist Maslow wrote that the greatest human need we have is to love and to be loved. But loving someone involves risk. We risk opening ourselves up to a wonderful world of happiness and fulfillment. But we also risk opening ourselves up for disappointment, rejection and pain.

Relationships in and of themselves are not good. Successful relationships with others take work in order to be healthy. They do not just happen. At the center of all successful relationships is love and respect. Healthy relationships are marked by equality—equal giving and receiving—or else you will find yourself in a co-dependent relationship. Healthy relationships are balanced ones and they add to our lives. Unhealthy relationships throw our lives off-balance and may cause trouble in other areas.

No one is perfect. We will experience troubles in relationships. Despite a person's best intentions (and no matter how much we love that person), there will be times when we are hurt by them. What will our response be when we are hurt? How will we respond at that time and how will we respond later? Can the relationship be restored to wholeness again or is the damage irreparable?

LEADER: Choose the OPTION 1 Bible Study (page 23) or the OPTION 2 Study (page 26).

In the Option 1 Study (from Matthew's Gospel), Jesus teaches Peter about forgiveness. In the Option 2 Study (from Paul's letter to the Romans), Paul describes a loving relationship between Christians and between non-Christians and Christians.

BIBLE STUDY / 30 Minutes / Groups of 4

Leader: Help the group decide on Option 1 or Option 2 for their Bible Study. If there are 7 or more in the group, encourage them to move into groups of 4. Ask one person in each group to be the Leader. The Leader guides the sharing and makes sure that each group member has an opportunity to answer every question.

Gospel Study / Forgive and Forget
Matthew 18:21–35

STUDY

This passage is known as the Parable of the Unmerciful Servant. In verses 15–20, the topics of sin, forgiveness and reconciliation are introduced. Here, this discussion is continued to get to the heart of the reason why the disciple of Jesus is to be merciful and forgiving toward others. Read Matthew 18:21–35 and discuss your responses to the following questions with the group.

21 Then Peter came to Jesus and asked, "Lord, how many times shall I forgive my brother when he sins against me? Up to seven times?"

22 Jesus answered, "I tell you, not seven times, but seventy-seven times.

23 "Therefore, the kingdom of heaven is like a king who wanted to settle accounts with his servants. 24 As he began the settlement, a man who owed him ten thousand talents was brought to him. 25 Since he was not able to pay, the master ordered that he and his wife and his children and all that he had be sold to repay the debt.

26 "The servant fell on his knees before him. 'Be patient with me,' he begged, 'and I will pay back everything.' 27 The servant's master took pity on him, canceled the debt and let him go.

28 "But when that servant went out, he found one of his fellow servants who owed him a hundred denarii. He grabbed him and began to choke him. 'Pay back what you owe me!' he demanded.

29 "His fellow servant fell to his knees and begged him, 'Be patient with me, and I will pay you back.'

30 "But he refused. Instead, he went off and had the man thrown into prison until he could pay the debt. 31 When the other servants saw what had happened, they were greatly distressed and went and told their master everything that had happened.

32 "Then the master called the servant in. 'You wicked servant,' he said, 'I canceled all that debt of yours because you begged me to. 33 Shouldn't you have had mercy on your fellow servant just as I had on you?' 34 In anger his master turned him over to the jailers to be tortured, until he should pay back all he owed.

35 "This is how my heavenly Father will treat each of you unless you forgive your brother from your heart."

Matthew 18:21–35, NIV

1. Which character in this parable do you most identify with?
   - ❏ the king (in the beginning of the story), because I'm really big-hearted
   - ❏ the first servant, because I'm in debt up to my ears
   - ❏ the first servant, because I'm angry at so-and-so (who is always borrowing from me, but never quite able to pay me back)
   - ❏ the second servant, because others always pick on me
   - ❏ the wife of the first servant, because my spouse is always getting us into trouble
   - ❏ the king (at the end of the story), because I hate it when I see injustice
   - ❏ the first servant (at the end of the story), because I can't believe how stupid I can be at times

2. Why do you think Peter asked this question about how many times he needed to forgive his brother?
   - ❏ Someone had just irritated him for the eighth time and he wanted to smack him.
   - ❏ He was the type to keep score.
   - ❏ He was really struggling with what it meant to forgive.
   - ❏ He wanted to have an answer for future reference.

3. Offenders in Jesus' day were forgiven up to three times; a fourth offense need not be forgiven. What does Jesus' answer say about forgiveness in the kingdom?
   - ❏ You have unlimited shots for forgiveness.
   - ❏ If you want forgiveness in your life, you had better be prepared to give it to others.
   - ❏ God keeps score and you have seventy-seven opportunities.
   - ❏ God's forgiveness is conditional and limited.
   - ❏ God's forgiveness is unconditional and unlimited.
   - ❏ God's forgiveness is conditional and unlimited.
   - ❏ other: _____

4. What is the principle for you (as a Christian) in dealing with someone who has wronged you?
   - ❏ You can't out-forgive God.
   - ❏ Scorekeepers end up getting hurt.
   - ❏ God expects you to be a "pushover."
   - ❏ You can take "an eye for an eye."
   - ❏ Don't let the scoundrel off the hook.
   - ❏ If you don't forgive others, God is going to refigure what you owe him.
   - ❏ People who don't forgive wind up in their own chains.
   - ❏ Only the forgiven know how to forgive.

"Doing an injury puts you below your enemy; revenging one makes you even with him; forgiving it sets you above him."
—Author unknown

5. Finish this sentence: "If we really took the teaching of this passage seriously today ..."
   ❏ all of the lending agencies would go out of business.
   ❏ people would think they could do anything and be forgiven.
   ❏ the world would have fewer bitter and unforgiving people.
   ❏ we would have a better understanding of all that God has forgiven us.
   ❏ people would be liberated, knowing they could put mistakes behind them.
   ❏ other: _____

6. What has helped you in dealing with someone who has hurt you?
   ❏ keeping short accounts
   ❏ writing a letter, but not mailing it
   ❏ asking someone else to mediate
   ❏ saying it straight out
   ❏ sleeping on it
   ❏ surprising them with a gift
   ❏ getting away from the situation
   ❏ ignoring it
   ❏ breaking off the friendship/relationship

7. Why do you think the servant in this parable was so unforgiving of his fellow servant?
   ❏ His parents were too strict when he was growing up.
   ❏ He needed the money for a party to celebrate.
   ❏ He was too self-focused.
   ❏ The Devil made him do it.
   ❏ He thought the other servant was less deserving of forgiveness.
   ❏ other: _____

8. Finish this sentence: "The person in my life who has been most like the king to me, forgiving me when I did not deserve it, has been ..."

9. Finish this sentence: "The person in my life who I have treated the most like the unmerciful servant treated his fellow servant is ..."

LEADER: When you have completed the Bible Study, move on to the Caring Time (page 30).

10. If you took the teaching of this parable seriously, what would be the first thing you would do?

❐ ask God to forgive that astronomical debt I owe

❐ forgive a certain person I have been unwilling to forgive

❐ say a special thanks to someone who extended forgiveness and mercy to me

❐ I'm already doing a good job of taking this seriously.

❐ I really don't want to take this seriously.

COMMENT

The rabbis taught that a person ought to be forgiven for a particular offense up to three times. After that, the offended person was under no obligation to grant forgiveness. Realizing that Jesus had a greater sense of the importance of mercy than was typical for rabbis, Peter was willing to double the traditional amount and add one more time for good measure! Since seven was considered the number of completion and perfection, Peter may have thought that anyone who could forgive someone that many times would be a spiritually perfect person.

OPTION 2

Epistle Study / Loving Relationships
Romans 12:9–21

STUDY

In this section of Paul's letter to the Romans, he describes relationships between Christians. In verses 14–21, he will conclude this section by discussing the question of how to relate to those who aren't Christians. Read Romans 12:9–21 and discuss your responses to the following questions with your group.

⁹Love must be sincere. Hate what is evil; cling to what is good. ¹⁰Be devoted to one another in brotherly love. Honor one another above yourselves. ¹¹Never be lacking in zeal, but keep your spiritual fervor, serving the Lord. ¹²Be joyful in hope, patient in affliction, faithful in prayer. ¹³Share with God's people who are in need. Practice hospitality.

¹⁴Bless those who persecute you; bless and do not curse. ¹⁵Rejoice with those who rejoice; mourn with those who mourn. ¹⁶Live in harmony with one another. Do not be proud, but be willing to associate with people of low position. Do not be conceited.

¹⁷Do not repay anyone evil for evil. Be careful to do what is right in the eyes of everybody. ¹⁸If it is possible, as far as it depends on you, live at peace with everyone. ¹⁹Do not take revenge, my friends, but leave room for God's wrath, for it is written: "It is mine to avenge; I will repay," says the Lord. ²⁰On the contrary:

"If your enemy is hungry, feed him;
if he is thirsty, give him something to drink.
In doing this, you will heap burning coals on his head."

²¹*Do not be overcome by evil, but overcome evil with good.*
Romans 12:9–21, NIV

1. Imagine that you were in the congregation at Rome and heard Paul's letter for the first time. What would be your initial reaction?
   ❏ Does he really expect us to do all this?
   ❏ Put down the pithy pen, Paul, and go back to theology.
   ❏ Isn't this the same guy who spoke against trying to live up to all the tenets of the Law?
   ❏ This is a high standard—I think I'll need some help.
   ❏ This is a challenging moral code which will help me to be my best and strive for holiness.

2. Which of Paul's admonitions do you have the most difficulty with?
   ❏ "honor one another above yourselves"—I'm trying to honor myself.
   ❏ "share with God's people who are in need"—They need to help themselves.
   ❏ "bless those who persecute you"—I'd rather punch them out.
   ❏ "do not be proud"—It's hard to be humble when you're perfect in every way.
   ❏ "be willing to associate with people of low position"—It's bad for my image.
   ❏ "live at peace with everyone"—You've got to be kidding.
   ❏ "do not take revenge"—I don't get mad; I get even.

3. Which of the above admonitions do you have the *easiest* time with?

4. Read the following descriptions by Paul about love. Which one do you find the most difficult to apply in your relationships?
   ❏ Love must be genuine—we shouldn't try to fake love, or to pretend to love others when we don't.
   ❏ Relate to others in the Christian community as if they were literally your brothers and sisters.
   ❏ This love will involve a devoted care and concern for the well-being of others.
   ❏ other: _____

5. In addition to love, Paul tells us other things we ought to do when we are in relationship with others. For each of the following, rate yourself on a scale of 1 to 5 (1 = "I need help with this" to 5 = "I'm doing well with this"):
    __I give honor to others.
    __I think about what others want and need before I think about myself.
    __I consider people worthy of honor because of who they are.
    __I do not minimize or look down on my brothers and sisters.
    __I gladly share with others.
    __I help my brothers and sisters when they have needs.
    __I practice the gift of hospitality to others—opening my home and my family to others.

6. What has been your usual way of reacting to persecution?
    ❑ crawling in a hole
    ❑ quietly developing an ulcer
    ❑ fighting fire with fire
    ❑ complaining to anyone who would listen
    ❑ mediation by a third party
    ❑ reporting the person to the proper authorities
    ❑ finding a way to return good for evil
    ❑ other: _____

7. Who do you have the greatest difficulty living at peace with at this time in your life?
    ❑ myself   ❑ my boss
    ❑ my spouse   ❑ my kids
    ❑ my parents   ❑ a rival at work
    ❑ someone in the church   ❑ a neighbor
    ❑ a friend   ❑ other: _____

8. What is your next step with the person who has "persecuted" you (or with whom you have the greatest difficulty)?
    ❑ I still say—punch them out.
    ❑ find a mediator
    ❑ take it to God in prayer
    ❑ find a way to "bless" them through an act of love
    ❑ wait for God to take revenge for me
    ❑ other: _____

"Any deep relationship to another human being requires watchfulness and nourishment; otherwise, it is taken from us. And we cannot recapture it. This is a form of having and not having that is the root of innumerable tragedies."
—Paul Tillich

9. Christians are instructed to respond to non-Christians in specific ways. Which of the following ways do you think are the most effective as you deal with non-Christians?

   ❏ They must offer a blessing in the face of hostility.

   ❏ When their enemies experience joy or success, Christians should join in the rejoicing and not begrudge them this joy (because they, as Christians, had been mistreated).

   ❏ They are to do all they can to promote peace and harmony.

   ❏ They are not to be haughty in their response—"You can't hurt me. I'm better than you."

   ❏ They are not to find someone lower than themselves to lord it over.

   ❏ Revenge and wrath must be left to God.

   ❏ They must respond to an enemy in need with acts of love.

   ❏ They should not choose the way of evil in order to fight evil.

LEADER: When you have completed the Bible Study, move on to the Caring Time (page 30).

10. Based on verses 9–13, rate your small group's experience by using the inventory below:

    ❏ LOVE TEST: We can be totally honest and open with each other in a spirit of love.

    ❏ GOODNESS TEST: We can share our struggles to "be God's people" with one another without fear or embarrassment.

    ❏ BROTHERLY LOVE TEST: We have a bond of love for each other like a family.

    ❏ HONOR TEST: We build up one another and consider each other's interests above our own.

    ❏ ZEAL TEST: We encourage one another to keep spiritually alive—red-hot in our spiritual faith.

    ❏ JOY, PATIENCE AND FAITHFULNESS TEST: We are committed to support each other through personal trials, tribulations and hardships.

    ❏ HOSPITALITY TEST: We are open to being a hostel—not only for each other, but also for hurting people who need a place to stay or belong.

CARING TIME / 15–45 Minutes / All Together

Leader: Bring all of the foursomes back together for a time of caring. Follow the Sharing, Prayer and Action paragraphs below. Be sensitive to what each one is sharing.

SHARING

Finish this sentence:

"The relationship in my life that God is asking me to work on is ..."

PRAYER

Remembering the requests which were just shared, close with a prayer time. The Leader can start a conversational prayer (short phrases and sentences), with group members following. After an appropriate amount of time, the Leader can close the time of prayer by praying for any requests not already mentioned.

ACTION

1. Plan one or two concrete steps you can take this week to help yourself grow in the relationship with the person you mentioned in prayer.

2. Choose one or two of the verses from one of the passages of Scripture in this study which has special meaning to you. Write the verses on a 3" x 5" card and place it somewhere where you will see it throughout the week.

SESSION 4

When Stress Builds

PURPOSE To develop helpful strategies when stress becomes troubling in our lives.

AGENDA  Gathering Bible Study Caring Time

OPEN **GATHERING / 15 Minutes / All Together**

Leader: Read the instructions for Step One and set the pace by going first. Then read the Introduction in Step Two and move on to the Bible Study.

Step One: Test Your Strength. How well we remember being at the county fair or circus and seeing young guys trying to impress their girl-friends with the "Test Your Strength" game. This is the game where they took a huge hammer and tried to hit a pad hard enough to force the weight up the meter and ring a bell.

This is one game where you don't want to hit the bell of 150 points. So step right up and give it your best shot! Circle the events you have experienced within the past year. Total your score. If it's more than 150 points, you're probably living under a lot of stress. (If you feel comfortable, share your score with the group.)

EVENT	STRESS POINTS	EVENT	STRESS POINTS
Death of spouse	100	Change in financial state	38
Divorce	73	Death of a close friend	37
Marital separation	65	Change in line of work	36
Jail term	63	Arguments with spouse	35
Death of family member	63	Large mortgage taken out	31
Personal injury or illness	53	Foreclosure on mortgage/loan	30
Marriage	50	Change in work	29
Loss of job	47	Son/daughter leaves home	29
Retirement	47	Trouble with in-laws	29
Marital reconciliation	45	Major achievement	28
Health Problem	44	Spouse starts/stops work	26
Pregnancy	40	Changes in living conditions	25
Sex difficulties	39	Revision of personal habits	24
Gain of new family member	39	Trouble with boss	23
Business readjustment	39	Change in work hours	20

Your Total _____

Step Two: When Stress Builds. We have become almost obsessed with stress in America. Pick up any popular magazine, turn on any talk show, read a newspaper, and chances are you will find something on stress and stress management.

Have we really become a more stressful people? Or are we simply more aware of our stress? Probably both are true to some degree. Our society today moves at a faster pace than years ago. We have increased demands on our time. Women are returning to the workforce in record numbers, while maintaining most of their household responsibilities. Parents who remain home with their families have increasing demands as children become more involved in activities, both in and out of school. Many people are working two jobs or longer hours on their job.

Financial pressures have certainly increased with higher prices of goods and services, requiring two working adults in most families. People are more concerned about health care costs, their own health and their long-term financial security.

Handling all that life gives us is a delicate balancing act. We want to have it all—not necessarily speaking exclusively of material possessions. But we want to have material things, plus a fulfilling career, friends, active social lives, enriched spiritual lives, time for ourselves—a private life, community involvement and the list goes on. Trying to balance all of these items (along with a normal dose of troubles) can lead to stress overload and burnout.

Burnout is a state of physical, intellectual, emotional and spiritual exhaustion. In our society, it has reached almost epidemic proportions. It is most evident in people in the helping professions—nurses, social workers, teachers, doctors and ministers. None of us are immune from the debilitating effects of burnout. Parents burn out from the pressures of providing for their families; singles can burn out from trying to do it all.

LEADER: Choose the OPTION 1 Bible Study (page 33) or the OPTION 2 Study (page 35).

In our Option 1 Study (from Luke's Gospel), we will study how Jesus tries to help Mary and Martha discover what's important in their lives. In the Option 2 Study (from Paul's second letter to the Corinthians), we will learn from Paul's example how to handle hardship, pressure, stress and distress.

BIBLE STUDY / 30 Minutes / Groups of 4

Leader: Help the group decide on Option 1 or Option 2 for their Bible Study. If there are 7 or more in the group, encourage them to move into groups of 4. Ask one person in each group to be the Leader. The Leader guides the sharing and makes sure that each group member has an opportunity to answer every question.

OPTION 1

Gospel Study / Too Busy
Luke 10:38–42

STUDY

In this passage, Jesus visits the home of his friends, Mary and Martha, and helps them to establish healthy priorities. Read Luke 10:38–42 and discuss your responses to the following questions with your group.

[38]As Jesus and his disciples were on their way, he came to a village where a woman named Martha opened her home to him. [39]She had a sister called Mary, who sat at the Lord's feet listening to what he said. [40]But Martha was distracted by all the preparations that had to be made. She came to him and asked, "Lord, don't you care that my sister has left me to do the work by myself? Tell her to help me!"

[41]"Martha, Martha," the Lord answered, "you are worried and upset about many things, [42]but only one thing is needed. Mary has chosen what is better, and it will not be taken away from her."

Luke 10:38–42, NIV

1. Growing up, who did you admire for the way they handled stress?
   - ❑ my mother
   - ❑ a grandparent
   - ❑ my pastor
   - ❑ another relative
   - ❑ a neighbor
   - ❑ my father
   - ❑ a brother/sister
   - ❑ a friend
   - ❑ a teacher
   - ❑ other: _____

2. Which of these situations quickly elevates your stress level?
   - ❑ a visit from a relative
   - ❑ seven straight days of rain
   - ❑ six hours in the car with my kids
   - ❑ my spouse asking me to help clean the house
   - ❑ my boss wanting to see me
   - ❑ sitting down to pay the monthly bills
   - ❑ other: _____

33

3. Why do you think Martha drove herself like she did?
   - ❐ She had a desire to prove herself.
   - ❐ It was the only way she could feel good about herself.
   - ❐ She loved Jesus.
   - ❐ She wanted to make an impression on Jesus.
   - ❐ It was a way to make herself look better than her sister Mary.

4. What Jesus was saying to Martha was:
   - ❐ She should chill out.
   - ❐ She should be more like Mary.
   - ❐ She could learn from Mary's different style.
   - ❐ She should be glad Mary had chosen to follow Christ.
   - ❐ other: _____

5. How do you feel about Jesus' response to Martha?
   - ❐ irritated—It just shows that he was a man with male values.
   - ❐ disappointed—He should have sent Mary in to help, so both could return to listen later when the work was done.
   - ❐ ambivalent—I see his point, but I don't like it.
   - ❐ justified—He approved the course I would have taken.
   - ❐ enlightened—He affirmed her need to receive from God rather than to endlessly strive on her own.

6. Why do you work hard? (choose two)
   - ❐ to please others
   - ❐ to fulfill a calling
   - ❐ to feel good about myself
   - ❐ to avoid relationships and responsibilities
   - ❐ I have a fear of failure.
   - ❐ I don't know how to slow down.
   - ❐ I'm driven by the desire to be successful.
   - ❐ I don't work all that hard.
   - ❐ other: _____

7. How would you compare your work habits with Martha's habits?
   - ❐ Our work habits are very similar.
   - ❐ Martha is a lot more driven than I am.
   - ❐ I'm a lot more driven than Martha.
   - ❐ It all depends on what work I'm doing.

"It is not the outward storms and stresses of life that defeat and disrupt personality, but its inner conflicts and miseries. If a man is happy and stable at heart, he can normally cope, even with zest, with difficulties that lie outside his personality."
—J.B. Phillips

34

8. On a scale of 1 to 10 (1 = very relaxed and 10 = very tense), give Mary, Martha, and yourself a number on each trait. If you score over 50 points, you may be prone to stress based on your personality.

"It's not enough to be busy ... the question is: What are we busy about?"
—Henry David Thoreau

MARY	MARTHA	ME	
_____	_____	_____	very competitive
_____	_____	_____	driving, forceful personality
_____	_____	_____	must succeed in everything
_____	_____	_____	have to get things done quickly
_____	_____	_____	anxious about what others think
_____	_____	_____	easily angered by people/things
_____	_____	_____	will do anything for public recognition
_____	_____	_____	very conscious of deadlines
_____	_____	_____	anxious about social advancement
_____	_____	_____	overloaded with activities
_____	_____	_____	high desire for popularity
_____	_____	_____	impatient when held back or delayed
_____	_____	_____	**TOTAL**

LEADER: When you have completed the Bible Study, move on to the Caring Time (page 38).

9. What "one thing is needed" for you to start taking the stress out of your life?
   ❒ I need to find a "Martha" to do all my work for me.
   ❒ I need to take on Mary's reflective, contemplative style.
   ❒ I need to learn more about Christ and what he thought was important in life.
   ❒ I need to be closer to Christ personally.
   ❒ other: _____

OPTION 2

Epistle Study / Overcoming Overload
2 Corinthians 1:3–11

STUDY

The apostle Paul had to undergo great hardships to establish some churches. One of those churches was in Corinth. In this passage, he reminds them of some of his experiences. Read this passage and discuss your responses to the following questions with your group.

³Praise be to the God and Father of our Lord Jesus Christ, the Father of compassion and the God of all comfort, ⁴who comforts us in all our troubles, so that we can comfort those in any trouble with the comfort we ourselves have received from God. ⁵For just as the sufferings of Christ flow over into our lives, so also through Christ our comfort overflows. ⁶If we are distressed, it is for your comfort and salvation; if we are comforted, it is for your comfort, which produces in you patient endurance of the same sufferings we suffer. ⁷And our hope for you is firm, because we know that just as you share in our sufferings, so also you share in our comfort.

⁸We do not want you to be uninformed, brothers, about the hardships we suffered in the province of Asia. We were under great pressure, far beyond our ability to endure, so that we despaired even of life. ⁹Indeed, in our hearts we felt the sentence of death. But this happened that we might not rely on ourselves but on God, who raises the dead. ¹⁰He has delivered us from such a deadly peril, and he will deliver us. On him we have set our hope that he will continue to deliver us, ¹¹as you help us by your prayers. Then many will give thanks on our behalf for the gracious favor granted us in answer to the prayers of many.

2 Corinthians 1:3–11, NIV

1. Imagine that you were a recipient of this letter. What would you have asked Paul the first time you saw him after hearing these words?
    ❑ What were the hardships in Asia all about?
    ❑ Why is your hope for us so firm?
    ❑ Why do you go through all of this for us?
    ❑ How can you always praise God when things get hard?
    ❑ How do you really handle all this stress?

2. What does Paul mean in saying, "For just as the sufferings of Christ flow over into our lives, so also through Christ our comfort overflows"?
    ❑ We suffer because of following Christ, but we also find comfort in heaven because of him.
    ❑ In Christ's fellowship, all is shared—the bad as well as the good.
    ❑ God has an overabundance of blessings in store for us if we follow Christ.
    ❑ Christ's suffering was followed by victory—so it will be with us.

3. When you were upset as a child, who comforted you?
    ❑ my mother/father   ❑ my best friend
    ❑ my grandparents   ❑ I didn't turn to anyone for comfort.
    ❑ my sister/brother   ❑ other: _____

4. Because God comforts us, we can comfort other people. How would you try to comfort someone who was deeply troubled?
   ❏ I'd listen to them.
   ❏ I'd pray for/with them.
   ❏ I'd tell them God will take care of them.
   ❏ I'd tell them that they need more faith.
   ❏ I'd tell them that they need to take control of their life.
   ❏ I wouldn't feel comfortable doing this.
   ❏ other: _____

5. What effect can stress or distress have in a Christian's life?
   ❏ Christians don't have stress in their lives.
   ❏ Stress makes a Christian dependent upon God.
   ❏ Stress makes a Christian overly dependent upon others.
   ❏ Stress causes one to question their faith.
   ❏ other: _____

6. When have you experienced what Paul did in verses 8 and 9—suffered hardships, been under great pressure, despaired of life?
   ❏ in my family growing up   ❏ during a particular job
   ❏ after a tragedy   ❏ during an illness
   ❏ in college/the military   ❏ other: _____
   ❏ recently

7. What does this passage say to you about your attitude when the stress in your life becomes overwhelming?
   ❏ If Paul made it through, so can I.
   ❏ I need to rely more on God and less on myself.
   ❏ God is trying to teach me something here.
   ❏ I need to see how what I'm going through can help someone else.
   ❏ If I'm going to share in Christ's rewards, I must share in his suffering and trials.
   ❏ Real Christians don't get distressed.
   ❏ other: _____

8. Often we do not recognize overload until we are too worn down to do much about it. The following exercise will help you determine if you are currently experiencing overload. If you feel comfortable, share your results with the group. Instructions: Indicate how frequently you experience each of the following statements. Use the scale below to rate each statement (0 = almost never, 1 = infrequently, 2 = frequently, 3 = almost always):

   __I am irritable with others (family, coworkers, etc.).
   __I feel emotionally drained by my work.
   __I have difficulty falling asleep at night.

___I lack motivation in my work.

___I am disillusioned with my work (including housework).

___I think, "Why don't people leave me alone?"

___I treat people more impersonally than I would like.

___I wake up tired and have difficulty facing another day.

___I consider myself a failure.

___I am bothered by stress-related ailments (such as indigestion, headaches, high blood pressure, etc.).

___I feel like I am at the end of my rope.

___I feel trapped in my work.

___I feel exhausted at the end of a workday.

___I feel people make a lot of demands on me.

___I feel unfulfilled and am dissatisfied with my life.

___TOTAL

LEADER: When you have completed the Bible Study, move on to the Caring Time (below).

Total your score. A score of 0–15 indicates that you are probably not experiencing overload. A score of 16–30 indicates that you are probably experiencing moderate overload (and should do something about it). A score of 31–45 indicates that you are probably experiencing severe overload (and definitely should do something about it).

 ## CARING TIME / 15–45 Minutes / All Together

Leader: Bring all of the foursomes back together for a time of caring support through Sharing, Prayer and Action.

SHARING

Share one situation you think you will face in the coming week where you will especially need God's help in dealing with your stress level.

PRAYER

During your time of prayer, remember the person next to you and what they shared about the coming week. You may say your prayer in silence, ending with a verbal "Amen," so the next person will know when to start.

ACTION

Remember your neighbor's prayer request throughout the week. Drop him/her a note of encouragement with respect to their prayer request.

SESSION 5
When You Fail

PURPOSE | To understand that failure is often a prerequisite for success.

AGENDA |  **Gathering**   **Bible Study**   **Caring Time**

OPEN | ## GATHERING / 15 Minutes / All Together

Leader: Read the Instructions for Step One and go first. Then read the Introduction (Step Two) and explain the Bible Study choices.

Step One: Things That Drive You Crazy. Take a moment and check the appropriate response to the following things which drive people crazy. How do you respond to them? Share your choices with the group.

	YES	NO	SOMETIMES
slow driver in the fast lane	❒	❒	❒
bathtub rings that aren't yours	❒	❒	❒
last page of your book is missing	❒	❒	❒
dripping faucet	❒	❒	❒
someone talking during a movie	❒	❒	❒
radio blaring in public	❒	❒	❒
losing one sock	❒	❒	❒
not enough toilet paper	❒	❒	❒
friend who is always late	❒	❒	❒
person who sings through a concert	❒	❒	❒
toothpaste squeezed in the middle	❒	❒	❒
preempting of television program	❒	❒	❒
an itch you can't reach	❒	❒	❒
screeching chalk on blackboard	❒	❒	❒
pen that will not work	❒	❒	❒
people that crack their gum	❒	❒	❒
back-seat driver	❒	❒	❒

Step Two: When You Fail. Success in life is the goal for many. And for some people it is their only goal in life. We often view success as the opposite of failure; in fact, success is often the by-product or end result of failure. All of us have failed at one time or another. And granted, it isn't much fun to fail. But if we fear failure, we can be immobilized and avoid anything which involves any degree of risk.

Since we know that each of us will fail, the key is to discover what to do when we fail. We need to develop skills on how to handle failure, as opposed to trying to discover ways to avoid failure. The stories of successful people invariably tell us that they have failed one or more times before they became successful. Thomas Edison failed repeatedly before he lit his first incandescent light bulb. Marie Curie persevered despite financial, scientific and health setbacks. Winston Churchill gave a perspective on failure when he said, "Success is going from failure to failure without loss of enthusiasm."

But if we are honest with ourselves, failure is very troubling to us. We feel inadequate because often our identity is tied to our failure. Some failures make us feel inferior to others, or indicate that we will never amount to anything in life.

LEADER:
Choose the
OPTION 1 Bible
Study (below)
or the OPTION 2
Study (page 43).

In the Option 1 Study (from the Gospel of Luke), Peter painfully learns some deeper truths through failure. In the Option 2 Study (from Paul's first letter to Timothy), Paul encourages Timothy to keep the faith despite his failures. Both studies will help us to rise above failure. Remember, the purpose of the Bible Study is to share your story. Use this opportunity to deal with issues in your life in this support group.

 BIBLE STUDY / 30 Minutes / Groups of 4

Leader: Help the group choose an Option for study. Divide into groups of 4 for discussion. Remind the Leader for each foursome to move the group along so the Bible Study can be completed in the time allotted. Ask everyone to return together for the Caring Time for the final 15–45 minutes.

OPTION 1

Gospel Study / Down, But Not Out
Luke 22:54–62

STUDY

Read Luke 22:54–62 and discuss your response to the following questions with your group. This story describes the experience of one of Jesus' disciples on the night that Jesus was arrested and taken away to be crucified.

⁵⁴Then seizing him [Jesus]**, they** [the temple police] **led him away and took him into the house of the high priest. Peter followed at a distance. ⁵⁵But when they had kindled a fire in the middle of the courtyard and had sat down together, Peter sat down with them. ⁵⁶A servant girl saw him seated there in the firelight. She looked closely at him and said, "This man was with him."**

⁵⁷But he denied it. "Woman, I don't know him," he said.

⁵⁸A little later someone else saw him and said, "You also are one of them."

"Man, I am not!" Peter replied.

⁵⁹About an hour later another asserted, "Certainly this fellow was with him, for he is a Galilean."

⁶⁰Peter replied, "Man, I don't know what you're talking about!" Just as he was speaking, the rooster crowed. ⁶¹The Lord turned and looked straight at Peter. Then Peter remembered the word the Lord had spoken to him: "Before the rooster crows today, you will disown me three times." ⁶²And he went outside and wept bitterly.

Luke 22:54–62, NIV

> *"Often we assume that God is unable to work in spite of our weaknesses, mistakes, and sins. We forget that God is a specialist; he is able to work our failures into his plans."*
> —Erwin W. Lutzer

1. Reflecting on this event, what good word would you put in for Peter?
    - ❒ He meant well.
    - ❒ He couldn't help it.
    - ❒ He came back.
    - ❒ He's only human.
    - ❒ He was confused.
    - ❒ He was only protecting himself.
    - ❒ I wouldn't have done any better.
    - ❒ other: _____

2. Why did Peter keep at a distance and repeatedly deny his association with Jesus?
    - ❒ He didn't want to get involved.
    - ❒ He didn't want to get into trouble with the authorities.
    - ❒ He was confused by who Jesus was.
    - ❒ He was trying to devise an escape plan.

3. If you were in Peter's shoes, how would you have reacted?
    - ❒ I would have kept my mouth shut.
    - ❒ I would have gone home.
    - ❒ I would have done the same as Peter.
    - ❒ I would have argued Jesus' case.
    - ❒ other: _____

4. How do you think Peter felt when Jesus looked at him?
   - ❑ He realized how stupid he had been.
   - ❑ He felt ashamed of his behavior.
   - ❑ He feared that Jesus would never forgive him.
   - ❑ He was unaffected by the whole matter.
   - ❑ He was humiliated by his failure.

"Simon Peter, the Rock, very often looked more like a sandpile than a rock."
—John Powell

5. What failure in your life comes closest to hitting you emotionally like Peter's failure hit him?
   - ❑ when I was divorced
   - ❑ when I went through bankruptcy
   - ❑ when I "fell off the wagon"
   - ❑ when I had a chance to talk about Christ, but I didn't
   - ❑ when I was unfaithful to my spouse
   - ❑ when I deceived my parents as an adolescent
   - ❑ when I was fired
   - ❑ other: _____

6. When you experience failure, whose face do you see in your mind (looking at you as Christ looked at Peter)?
   - ❑ my father's
   - ❑ my mother's
   - ❑ my grandparent's
   - ❑ my old teacher's
   - ❑ Christ's
   - ❑ I've never experienced this.
   - ❑ a friend's
   - ❑ other: _____

LEADER: When you have completed the Bible Study, move on to the Caring Time (page 45).

7. How has failure in your life changed you?
   - ❑ I am now more caring and empathetic.
   - ❑ I am now more determined than ever.
   - ❑ I am now more humble.
   - ❑ I now look out for myself more.
   - ❑ I am now more realistic.
   - ❑ I am now emotionally fragile.
   - ❑ I am now confused and disillusioned.
   - ❑ I am now wiser.
   - ❑ other: _____

8. What lesson or principle would you like to pass on to your kids in dealing with failure?

Talk about failure ... It was bad enough that Peter denied Jesus, but worse coming right on the heels of his boast: "Even if I have to die with you, I will never disown you" (Mark 14:31). However, it is probably this experience that opened Peter's eyes to himself and made it possible for him to come to Jesus in repentance and faith. His failure did not affect his relationship with Jesus. The angel at the tomb makes a point of saying, "Go, tell his disciples and Peter, 'He is going ahead of you into Galilee. There you will see him' " (Mark 16:7). His failure did not affect Peter's role in the church. He became one of its pillars (Gal. 2:7–9). For the Christian, failure is not the end. It is often the beginning of new ministry, because it is in our weakness that we are made strong (Rom. 8:26; 1 Cor. 2:1; 2 Cor 12:7–10).

OPTION 2

Epistle Study / God's Grace for All
1 Timothy 1:12–20

STUDY

Paul's recollection that "the glorious gospel" had been "entrusted" to him leads him into this description of God's grace. Perhaps this is a gentle encouragement for Timothy not to despair. Read 1 Timothy 1:12–20 and discuss your responses to the following questions with your group.

12I thank Christ Jesus our Lord, who has given me strength, that he considered me faithful, appointing me to his service. 13Even though I was once a blasphemer and a persecutor and a violent man, I was shown mercy because I acted in ignorance and unbelief. 14The grace of our Lord was poured out on me abundantly, along with the faith and love that are in Christ Jesus.

15Here is a trustworthy saying that deserves full acceptance: Christ Jesus came into the world to save sinners—of whom I am the worst. 16But for that very reason I was shown mercy so that in me, the worst of sinners, Christ Jesus might display his unlimited patience as an example for those who would believe on him and receive eternal life. 17Now to the King eternal, immortal, invisible, the only God, be honor and glory for ever and ever. Amen.

18Timothy, my son, I give you this instruction in keeping with the prophecies once made about you, so that by following them you may fight the good fight, 19holding on to faith and a good conscience. Some have rejected these and so have shipwrecked their faith. 20Among them are Hymenaeus and Alexander, whom I have handed over to Satan to be taught not to blaspheme.

1 Timothy 1:12–20, NIV

1. Describe your first reaction to the teaching of this passage.
    - ❐ Paul is really too hard on himself.
    - ❐ Paul is very distraught.
    - ❐ Paul must be emotionally drained.
    - ❐ What great words of hope and encouragement.
    - ❐ I wish "so-and-so" could hear this.

2. If you could give someone who is "a failure" a word of advice based on your experience, what would you say?
   ❑ It's all right to admit your failures, but don't dwell on them.
   ❑ Try to concentrate on God's grace, and less on your failures.
   ❑ This is beyond me.
   ❑ other: _____

3. Paul spoke of Christ's "unlimited patience" with him. Having read verse 13 of this passage, how patient would you have been with Paul?
   ❑ not at all—I say, "The more people change, the more they stay the same."
   ❑ not very—About as patient as I am with his long, complicated letters.
   ❑ some—I am aware of a few successful turnaround stories.
   ❑ a lot—The best Christians are those who once were rebellious.

"Failure sometimes enlarges the spirit. You have to fall back upon humanity and God."
—Charles H. Cooley

4. Paul considers himself a chief sinner, but he was appointed by Christ for service. How do Paul's words affect your self-image?
   ❑ If Paul considers himself a chief sinner—that puts me in big trouble.
   ❑ I think Paul is overestimating his usefulness to Christ.
   ❑ I guess there's no hope for me.
   ❑ I guess there is hope for me.

5. On the following scale, how would you rate your self-perception in regard to moral failure?

1	2	3	4	5	6	7	8	9	10
"the worst of sinners"				about like most people					better than most people

6. Which failure in life do you fear the most?
   ❑ failing my family/friends   ❑ failing God in my faith
   ❑ failing financially   ❑ failing socially
   ❑ personal emotional failure   ❑ other: _____

7. On which of the following might you "shipwreck" your faith?
   ❑ the "rocks" of hard times
   ❑ the "shallows" of pleasures that lure me away from spiritual life
   ❑ an "iceberg" of spiritual or relational coldness
   ❑ crashing into another ship in the "fog" of uncertain spiritual direction
   ❑ My faith is shipwreck-proof.

LEADER: When you have completed the Bible Study, move on to the Caring Time (below).

8. What do you need to do to avoid such a shipwreck?
    - ❐ keep focused on the "lighthouse" of God's Word
    - ❐ always have the "anchor" of faith ready
    - ❐ rely on the support of my "sailing crew" who struggle with me
    - ❐ keep Christ as the "Captain" of my ship
    - ❐ avoid sailing into the "storms" of temptation

9. How does Paul establish both his humility and his authority?
    - ❐ He admits his failures and his need for Christ.
    - ❐ He affirms his gifts and abilities while still admitting his failures.
    - ❐ His central theme is one of God's grace through Christ.
    - ❐ He relies on his experiences of failure and faith.

10. How has God shown his unlimited patience with you?

COMMENT

There is an inner principle in all people that inclines them to failure. Failure is normal; success is the surprise. Here Paul identifies the reason for this: it is sin dwelling in us. And the word "sin" in the New Testament refers not just to active transgression, but also to falling short of what should be (i.e., failure). But Paul does not end with this fact. He highlights God's grace and love through the person and work of Jesus Christ to balance the failure in our lives.

 # CARING TIME / 15–45 Minutes / All Together

Leader: Bring all of the foursomes back together for a time of caring. Follow the Sharing, Prayer and Action paragraphs below.

SHARING

If you were to review your life and pinpoint "failures" that have crippled you, where would you begin? Is this something you have to deal with? Is this something that this group could help you deal with? If anybody wants to share, give them your heart.

Before you move into prayer, go around and let everyone finish the sentence:

"The one area of my life where I could use the help of someone is ..."

PRAYER

During your time of prayer, remember the person next to you and what they shared. You may pray in silence, ending with a verbal "Amen," so that the next person will know when to start.

ACTION

This week affirm God's grace and love in your life. Write down on a piece of paper one or two times in your life where you have failed. Destroy the paper, symbolizing that you're giving these failures to God once and for all. Then thank God for his grace in your life.

SESSION 6
When Tragedy Strikes

PURPOSE To develop helpful strategies for survival tragedies.

AGENDA  **Gathering**   **Bible Study**   **Caring Time**

OPEN   **GATHERING / 15 Minutes / All Together**

Leader: Read the instructions for Step One and go first. Then read the Introduction (Step Two) and explain the choices for Bible Study.

Step One: Past, Present and Future. Take a few moments to look back into your past, investigate the present, and take a glance at the future. Share your answers with the group.

Past: If I were young again, I would spend more time:
- ❏ reading great books
- ❏ talking about ...
- ❏ with my family
- ❏ getting involved in church
- ❏ loving my friends
- ❏ praying
- ❏ playing
- ❏ working in community projects
- ❏ stopping to smell the flowers
- ❏ other: _____

Present: Life would be better if there were more:
- ❏ parades
- ❏ country fairs
- ❏ Sunday dinners
- ❏ corner druggists
- ❏ homemade bread
- ❏ egg hunts
- ❏ family picnics
- ❏ carnivals and circuses
- ❏ revivals
- ❏ mom and pop stores
- ❏ square dances
- ❏ other: _____

Future: When I am 100 years old, I hope I am still able to:
- ❏ make love
- ❏ grow flowers
- ❏ play with children
- ❏ make people laugh
- ❏ go on a date
- ❏ take a joke
- ❏ think creatively
- ❏ drive a car
- ❏ take care of myself
- ❏ walk a mile
- ❏ play a sport
- ❏ listen to rock music
- ❏ earn a living
- ❏ other: _____

Step Two: When Tragedy Strikes. We all experience troubles in our lives. And we all have some skills in dealing with the day-to-day hassles and problems. For most of us, these troubles do not shake our faith to its core. We may find ourselves bending a bit to the winds of trouble, but we can hold steady to the course, and weather the storm until we get to the other side of our problem.

But what do we do when tragedy strikes? How do we handle the big losses in our lives—problems such as a major illness, a business failure, bankruptcy, or death? When we find our faith shaken to the core and we feel that God has deserted us, what do we do?

Death is the ultimate tragedy. There is no turning back. There are no second chances. And many times (despite the wonders of modern medicine) we are helpless when one we love is dying. How do we cope with the loss of control? How do we cope with such a loss? Part of coping is looking forward to the future, relying on what we know to be true about our faith and life in the hereafter.

The good news is that despite the particular tragedy, our faith offers us words of reassurance and hope. We are given hope for this life and for the life hereafter. There are many differences between the lives of Christians and non-Christians. No contrast is more stark than in death. For a person of faith, death is a transition from a troubled life on earth to an eternal life in God's presence.

LEADER:
Choose the
OPTION 1 Bible
Study (page 48)
or the OPTION 2
Study (page 50).

In Option 1 (from John's Gospel), we'll look at Jesus' words of hope for those who have died. Then in Option 2 (from Paul's second letter to the Corinthians), we will discover the importance of persevering, even when life's tragedies seem to be overwhelming.

 ## BIBLE STUDY / 30 Minutes / Groups of 4
Leader: Help the group choose an Option for study. Divide into groups of 4 for discussion. Remind the Leader for each foursome to move the group along so the Bible Study can be completed in the time allotted. Ask everyone to return together for the Caring Time for the final 15–45 minutes.

Gospel Study / Going Home
John 14:1–6

STUDY

In this passage, Jesus comforts his disciples about his upcoming death and the death each of them will face in the future. Read John 14:1–6 and discuss the questions that follow with your group.

14 *"Do not let your hearts be troubled. Trust in God; trust also in me. ²In my Father's house are many rooms; if it were not so, I would have told you. I am going there to prepare a place for you. ³And if I go and prepare a place for you, I will come back and take you to be with me that you also may be where I am. ⁴You know the way to the place where I am going.*

⁵Thomas said to him, "Lord, we don't know where you are going, so how can we know the way?"

⁶Jesus answered, "I am the way and the truth and the life. No one comes to the Father except through me."

John 14:1–6, NIV

"Think of sweeping on shore and finding it Heaven! Of taking hold of a hand and finding it God's! ... Of passing from storm and stress to a perfect calm. Of waking and finding it home!"
—Author unknown

1. What is your initial reaction to this description of what awaits us after death?
   - ❐ I hope they don't lose my reservation.
   - ❐ Sounds a little like "pie in the sky, by and by" to me.
   - ❐ This sounds too physical to me—I want a more spiritual reward.
   - ❐ The important part is I will have a special place prepared for me.
   - ❐ The important part is that I will be with Jesus.

2. How many rooms were in "your father's (or mother's) house" when you were a child? Which of those rooms was your favorite one, and why?

3. As a child, what was your first experience with death?
   - ❐ the death of a pet
   - ❐ the death of a grandparent
   - ❐ the death of a parent
   - ❐ the death of a sibling
   - ❐ the death of a childhood friend
   - ❐ other: _____

4. How did you handle the death in question #3?

5. Whose death has been hardest for you as an adult?

6. What kind of place would you like to have prepared for you in heaven?
   ❏ a place with lots of caring and loving people
   ❏ a place with some challenging things to do—and I don't mean playing the harp
   ❏ a place of comfort—to make up for my present deprivation
   ❏ a place with lots of natural beauty—like mountains and lakes
   ❏ a place with variety—wall-to-wall mansions might be boring
   ❏ a place of perfect knowledge, where everything makes sense

7. Jesus instructs his disciples (including us) to trust him. On a scale of 1 to 5, indicate below your ability to trust God in these matters:

1	2	3	4	5	6	7	8	9	10
I do not trust him.				I trust him somewhat.					I fully trust him.

   __with my family   __with my business/career
   __with my finances   __with my future
   __with illness   __with relationships/friends
   __with financial pressures   __with global concerns

8. Which of the above (from question #7) troubles your heart today?

LEADER: When you have completed the Bible Study, move on to the Caring Time (page 53).

9. What needs to be your next step along your faith journey?
   ❏ to learn to trust more, and control less
   ❏ to commit myself to Jesus as "the way"
   ❏ to face the reality of a death that has occurred in my life
   ❏ to open myself up to the hope of eternal life
   ❏ other: _____

COMMENT

If you have a few minutes remaining, read the following quote from Dwight L. Moody and reflect on it with other group members:

"Someday you will read in the papers that D. L. Moody of East Northfield is dead. Don't you believe a word of it. At that moment I shall be more alive than now. I shall have gone up higher, that is all—out of this old clay tenement into a house that is immortal; a body that death cannot touch, that sin cannot taint, a body fashioned like unto his glorious body. That which is born of the flesh may die. That which is born of the spirit will live forever."

Epistle Study / Perseverance
2 Corinthians 4:8–18

STUDY

Read 2 Corinthians 4:8–18 and share your responses to the following questions with your group. This is part of a message the apostle Paul wrote to the church in Corinth.

⁸We are hard pressed on every side, but not crushed; perplexed, but not in despair; ⁹persecuted, but not abandoned; struck down, but not destroyed. ¹⁰We always carry around in our body the death of Jesus, so that the life of Jesus may also be revealed in our body. ¹¹For we who are alive are always being given over to death for Jesus' sake, so that his life may be revealed in our mortal body. ¹²So then, death is at work in us, but life is at work in you.

¹³It is written: "I believed; therefore I have spoken." With that same spirit of faith we also believe and therefore speak, ¹⁴because we know that the one who raised the Lord Jesus from the dead will also raise us with Jesus and present us with you in his presence. ¹⁵All this is for your benefit, so that the grace that is reaching more and more people may cause thanksgiving to overflow to the glory of God.

¹⁶Therefore we do not lose heart. Though outwardly we are wasting away, yet inwardly we are being renewed day by day. ¹⁷For our light and momentary troubles are achieving for us an eternal glory that far outweighs them all. ¹⁸So we fix our eyes not on what is seen, but on what is unseen. For what is seen is temporary, but what is unseen is eternal.

2 Corinthians 4:8–18, NIV

1. If you didn't know this was from the Bible, what would it sound like to you?
   - ❒ the half time speech of a coach who is in a tough game
   - ❒ a letter home from a soldier on the front lines
   - ❒ instructions from a mystical guru
   - ❒ "spin control" by the press secretary of a candidate who is behind in the polls

2. When you were an adolescent, in which of these situations were you most likely to "rally from behind"?
   - ❒ playing sports
   - ❒ competing for a certain guy/girl
   - ❒ bringing my grades up after an early "D" or "F"
   - ❒ in trying out for a spot in the play against a more experienced person
   - ❒ in running for school office
   - ❒ other: _____

3. How good were you at "rallying from behind" when you were an adolescent?
   ❏ I was the "comeback kid."
   ❏ I could do it when I had to.
   ❏ I do remember a couple of times when I did it.
   ❏ When I got behind, it was all over but the crying.

4. These five categories of troubles are taken from this Scripture. Take a moment to check your stress factor. Put an "**✗**" on the line below—somewhere between "I'm fine with this" and "Panic Button."

   HASSLES: Minor crises at home/work, like car trouble, bills, speeding tickets, overdrawn checking account, etc.

   I'm fine with this _____ **Panic Button**

   DOUBTS: Inner turmoil about myself; what I really want to do in life; not achieving my life's goals; seeing my children fail, etc.

   I'm fine with this _____ **Panic Button**

   ENEMIES: Personal attacks on me; cheap shots from former friends, gossip, half-truths, betrayal, put-downs and letdowns, etc.

   I'm fine with this _____ **Panic Button**

   HURTS: Physical or emotional pain caused by tension, broken relationships, rejection, failure, disappointment, humiliation, etc.

   I'm fine with this _____ **Panic Button**

   TRAGEDIES: Troubles over which I have little (or no) control, such as a major illness, losing my job, war, death, etc.

   I'm fine with this _____ **Panic Button**

5. Which of the reasons that Paul suggests for "not losing heart" are most helpful to you with the troubles you face?
   ❏ The God who "raised Jesus from the dead" is with us (v. 14).
   ❏ Death cannot defeat us because God will raise us from death (v. 14).
   ❏ God uses our troubles for a greater good (v. 17).
   ❏ The troubles we see are temporary; the promises of God are unseen but eternal (v. 18).

"You and I were created for joy, and if we miss it, we miss the reason for our existence. ... If our joy is honest joy, it must somehow be congruous with human tragedy. This is the test of joy's integrity: is it compatible with pain? ... Only the heart that hurts has a right to joy."
—Lewis Smedes

6. Try to imagine yourself suffering the loss of one of the items below and having to continue with your life. Which item would you give up first? Which would you give up last? Rank this list in the order you would be able to do without (or suffer that loss) and still continue on with your life:

___my health: loss of physical coordination

___my savings: loss of money, stocks, and assets

___my possessions: loss of my house, clothes, etc.

___my country: loss of political freedom

___my career: loss of my job or job opportunity in the field of my choice

___my friends: loss of close relationships

___my family: loss of parents, spouse, siblings, or children

___my self-esteem: loss of self-worth, dignity, sense of importance

___my faith in God: loss of trust in the all-powerful, all-knowing God

___my integrity: loss of my values and character

___my reputation: loss of popularity, what others think of me

7. On the following scale, mark how important the resurrection of the dead was according to Paul with a "P," and how important it is to your faith with an "M":

Irrelevant	A secondary issue	A primary issue	Essential

LEADER: When you have completed the Bible Study, move on to the Caring Time (page 53).

8. Which of the following reasons to believe in Christ's resurrection do you find to be the most compelling?

   ❏ The Bible says it's true.

   ❏ The lives and attitudes of the disciples were radically turned around.

   ❏ The testimony of the Holy Spirit in my heart assures me.

   ❏ Christ's enemies could have disproved it by producing his body.

   ❏ The early disciples earnestly believed it—they died proclaiming it.

   ❏ None of the reasons above are compelling to me.

9. What do you need to do to cope with the painful issue of death?

   ❏ believe in my heart what I know in my head—that we will be made alive again

   ❏ talk more about an earlier death of a loved one

   ❏ work for something more permanent—not something that is just temporary

   ❏ learn more about Christ's victory over sin and death (vv. 14–15)

   ❏ accept Christ as my Lord and Savior

CARING TIME / 15–45 Minutes / All Together
Leader: Bring all of the foursomes back together for a time of caring support for each other through Sharing, Prayer and Action as found below.

SHARING

Indulge Yourself! Here is a chance for you to choose a way you can be good to yourself. Here's how it works: Review the list below and choose one thing that you will do for yourself before the next meeting. Take turns telling the group what you have chosen. At the next meeting, the group will ask you if you took care of yourself the way you planned.

Before our next meeting, I am going to take care of myself by:
- ❑ getting a massage
- ❑ taking a trip
- ❑ taking a personal retreat
- ❑ buying fresh-cut flowers
- ❑ having a slumber party
- ❑ getting a facial/manicure
- ❑ making my favorite dessert
- ❑ walking or running ___ miles
- ❑ buying new clothes
- ❑ praying for ___ minutes daily
- ❑ having a gourmet dinner
- ❑ buying the gadget I've wanted
- ❑ sitting by the pool and enjoying the sun
- ❑ organizing my closet/desk/bookshelves
- ❑ cutting out the TV/junk food/tobacco/alcohol
- ❑ grabbing a friend and doing something I've always wanted to do

PRAYER

Close with a time of prayer, remebering any requests that have been shared.

ACTION

On a 3" x 5" card, write the verses below and place the card somewhere where you will see it throughout the week:

> *Therefore, we do not lose heart. Though outwardly we are wasting away, yet inwardly we are being renewed day by day. For our light and momentary troubles are achieving for us an eternal glory that far outweighs them all. So we fix our eyes not on what is seen, but on what is unseen. For what is seen is temporary, but what is unseen is eternal.*
>
> *2 Corinthians 4:16–18*

SESSION 7
When Questions Remain

To reaffirm the eternal hope we have in Christ, even when we still have questions.

AGENDA

 Gathering   **Bible Study**   **Caring Time**

OPEN

 GATHERING / 15 Minutes / All Together

Leader: This is the final session together. You may want to have your Caring Time first. If not, be sure to allow a full 25 minutes at the end of the session.

Step One: A Trip to the Zoo. How would you describe your experience during this course with this group? Choose one of the animals below that best describes how your experience in this group affected your life. Then share your responses with the group.

WILD EAGLE: You have helped to heal my wings, and taught me how to soar again.

TOWERING GIRAFFE: You have helped me to hold my head up and stick my neck out, and reach over the fences I have built.

PLAYFUL PORPOISE: You have helped me to find a new freedom and a whole new world to play in.

COLORFUL PEACOCK: You have told me that I'm beautiful; I've started to believe it, and it's changing my life.

SAFARI ELEPHANT: I have enjoyed this new adventure, and I'm not going to forget it, or this group; I can hardly wait for the next safari.

LOVABLE HIPPOPOTAMUS: You have let me surface and bask in warm sunshine of God's love.

LANKY LEOPARD: You have helped me to look closely at myself an some spots, and you've told me it's okay to be this way.

DANCING BEAR: You have taught me to dance in the midst of pai you have helped me to reach out and hug again.

ALL-WEATHER DUCK: You have helped me to celebrate life— stormy weather—and to sing in the rain.

Step Two: When Questions Remain. Even people of great faith have questions which remain. "Why did my child have to die?" "Why is this happening to me?" "Doesn't God realize that I can't handle one more thing?" "Why do bad things happen to such good people?" "Why do people insist on fighting with each other?" "Doesn't he realize how much he is hurting the family by doing that?"

Sometimes we even have doubts about God and our faith. "Where has God gone?" "Why do I feel so alone?" One of the healthiest things we can do when those questions linger in our minds is to ask God about them. We need to ask God our questions and confess to him our doubts.

By verbalizing our questions to God, we are released from some of the fear of the unknown (and even the known). Then we are open to receive God's grace in our lives. As we receive God's grace anew, our hopes are renewed. More importantly, we are reminded that we won't go through our troubles alone. Christians do not receive special treatment from God, but they are assured that he will be with them every step of the way.

LEADER:
Choose the
OPTION 1 Bible
Study (below)
or the OPTION 2
Study (page 59).

In Option 1 (from Luke's Gospel), we will study the questions of the two disciples walking on the Emmaus road. The time is immediately following Christ's crucifixion, and they do not realize that he has been resurrected. And in Option 2 (from Paul's letter to the Romans), we will read the words of encouragement and hope for all people of faith.

BIBLE STUDY / 25 Minutes / Groups of 4

Leader: Remind the Leaders to end their Bible Study time five minutes earlier than usual to allow ample time for your final Caring Time—deciding what the group will do next.

OPTION 1

Gospel Study / Renewal of Hope
Luke 24:13–32

STUDY

Read Luke 24:13–32 and discuss your responses to the following questions with your group.

¹³Now that same day two of them were going to a village called Emmaus, about seven miles from Jerusalem. ¹⁴They were talking with each other about everything that had happened. ¹⁵As they talked and discussed these things with each other, Jesus himself came up and walked along with them; ¹⁶but they were kept from recognizing him.
¹⁷He asked them, "What are you discussing together as you walk along?" They stood still, their faces downcast. ¹⁸One of them, named Cleopas,

asked him, "Are you only a visitor to Jerusalem and do not know the things that have happened there in these days?"

[19]"What things?" he asked.

"About Jesus of Nazareth," they replied. "He was a prophet, powerful in word and deed before God and all the people. [20]The chief priests and our rulers handed him over to be sentenced to death, and they crucified him; [21]but we had hoped that he was the one who was going to redeem Israel. And what is more, it is the third day since all this took place. [22]In addition, some of our women amazed us. They went to the tomb early this morning [23]but didn't find his body. They came and told us that they had seen a vision of angels, who said he was alive. [24]Then some of our companions went to the tomb and found it just as the women had said, but him they did not see."

[25]He said to them, "How foolish you are, and how slow of heart to believe all that the prophets have spoken! [26]Did not the Christ have to suffer these things and then enter his glory?" [27]And beginning with Moses and all the Prophets, he explained to them what was said in all the Scriptures concerning himself.

[28]As they approached the village to which they were going, Jesus acted as if he were going farther. [29]But they urged him strongly, "Stay with us, for it is nearly evening; the day is almost over." So he went in to stay with them.

[30]When he was at table with them, he took bread, gave thanks, broke it and began to give it to them. [31]Then their eyes were opened and they recognized him, and he disappeared from their sight. [32]They asked each other, "Were not our hearts burning within us while he talked with us on the road and opened the Scriptures to us?"

Luke 24:13–32, NIV

1. If you were a reporter for *The Jerusalem Times* and interviewed these two men about their experience, which of these questions would you make sure to ask them?
   ❏ Have either of you ever been on drugs?
   ❏ How hot did you say the sun was?
   ❏ Do you always talk to strangers on dangerous and lonely roads?
   ❏ Why didn't you recognize Jesus at first?
   ❏ What did he mean about the Christ having to suffer?
   ❏ You say Jesus disappeared—couldn't he have walked awa[y] when you weren't looking?

2. Why do you think Jesus' followers left Jerusalem after they he[ard] that the body was missing?
   ❏ despair: "Everything I've lived for is gone."
   ❏ betrayal: "God has let me down."
   ❏ disillusionment: "I've been had."
   ❏ pain: "I can't take it anymore."
   ❏ abandoned: "I'm all alone now."
   ❏ withdrawal: "I'm getting away from it all."

3. Why didn't the men recognize Jesus when he joined them?
   - ❏ They refused to recognize what their mind said was impossible.
   - ❏ The disciples were preoccupied and weren't paying attention.
   - ❏ Jesus was invisible in his resurrection body.
   - ❏ They were miraculously kept from recognizing him.

4. Why might Jesus have been disappointed with these disciples?
   - ❏ They didn't believe the women's testimony.
   - ❏ They didn't understand the prophecies of Scripture.
   - ❏ They didn't recognize him when they saw him.
   - ❏ They had given up on their hope.

5. When do you think the healing started in their lives?
   - ❏ when they started to verbalize their disillusionment
   - ❏ when Jesus explained the Scripture to them
   - ❏ when their hearts started to "burn"
   - ❏ when they went back to the fellowship of the Upper Room and shared their story

6. What has God used to restore your faith and renew your spirit in times of great loss?
   - ❏ a fellowship of caring people
   - ❏ time away to be with God
   - ❏ talking out my pain with a trusted friend/counselor
   - ❏ I have never experienced the loss of hope to this degree.

7. How would you describe the road you are traveling along in life?
   - ❏ all uphill
   - ❏ a rocky and dusty road
   - ❏ a lonely road
   - ❏ a four-lane superhighway
   - ❏ a winding mountain road with great scenery
   - ❏ an easy country road lined with farms, where everyone knows each other
   - ❏ a detour where grass is growing in the middle of the path

8. Imagine that Jesus suddenly comes alongside you today and walks seven miles with you. What do you think he would talk about?
   - ❏ some of the troubles I'm experiencing right now
   - ❏ my job
   - ❏ my sense of financial panic
   - ❏ my anger with God over a personal tragedy
   - ❏ my disappointment in a relationship
   - ❏ my domestic problems/hassles
   - ❏ questions/doubts about my faith or church
   - ❏ my lack of direction from God
   - ❏ He probably wouldn't say a word. He would just be there.
   - ❏ I don't know. I really don't know.

LEADER: When you have completed the Bible Study, move on to the Caring Time (page 62).

9. What are you "slow of heart to believe" as you walk along that road?
   - ❐ that Jesus really is present with me
   - ❐ that this road actually goes somewhere
   - ❐ that lost hope can be found
   - ❐ that the road does not end in death

10. What would it take for you to recognize the presence of Christ in your life right now?
    - ❐ a special feeling—that "burning" in my heart
    - ❐ an obvious miracle
    - ❐ the elimination of my problems
    - ❐ a change in me—a willingness to commit to the "unseen"
    - ❐ I already recognize that presence.

COMMENT

Like these disciples, we also understand the experience of pinning our hopes on what we know is certain to take place in the future: a great job will materialize, a wonderful spouse will appear, our children will succeed. But it doesn't always happen that way. Someone else is offered the job; the person you love doesn't feel the same way about you; your child drops out of school and lives off others. What once seemed so bright is now dull and tarnished. The dreams die. Energy fades. Where once there was hope, now there is despair. Is there any way to recover hope?

In this story, the hope that was lost is that Jesus would redeem Israel; that he would fulfill all of God's promises to them; that they would once again become a great people. All of this was shattered by a Roman cross. But something happens to the two travelers. They who were "downcast" now feel their "hearts burning" within them. Hope rises again.

What happened? What brought about the change? In this passage, first they articulated what their hopes had been. Second, they found that the answer to their dashed hopes was there with them all along. They just did not see it yet. Third, their eyes were opened by Jesus. He gave them new hope.

There is insight for us here. It would be wrong to suggest that all loss and tragedy is merely a matter of not knowing the facts (in this case, that Jesus had been resurrected), and that things will be all right when the are made known. It is true, however, that the shock of the loss often p alyzes our vision so that we see only what we have lost, and not what have. We need new eyes to see our loss in its full context. How does new vision come? It comes from Jesus. He brings us words of w and insight (through Scripture and his people). It is he who also g the gift of life. His resurrection life is our resurrection life. As we tou life, we recover our life.

Epistle Study / Eternal Hope
Romans 8:18–25,31–39

STUDY

Christians in the early church had to deal with the reality of suffering. They were persecuted socially by the traditional religious leadership of the Jews, and later physically by the Roman government. In this passage, Paul tells the Christians at Rome that the sufferings we go through in this life are nothing compared to the joys that are in store for us. Read Romans 8:18–25,31–39 and discuss your responses to the following questions with your group.

[18]I consider that our present sufferings are not worth comparing with the glory that will be revealed in us. [19]The creation waits in eager expectation for the sons of God to be revealed. [20]For the creation was subjected to frustration, not by its own choice, but by the will of the one who subjected it, in hope [21]that the creation itself will be liberated from its bondage to decay and brought into the glorious freedom of the children of God.

[22]We know that the whole creation has been groaning as in the pains of childbirth right up to the present time. [23]Not only so, but we ourselves, who have the firstfruits of the Spirit, groan inwardly as we wait eagerly for our adoption as sons, the redemption of our bodies. [24]For in this hope we were saved. But hope that is seen is no hope at all. Who hopes for what he already has? [25]But if we hope for what we do not yet have, we wait for it patiently. ...

[31]What, then, shall we say in response to this? If God is for us, who can be against us? [32]He who did not spare his own Son, but gave him up for us all—how will he not also, along with him, graciously give us all things? [33]Who will bring any charge against those whom God has chosen? It is God who justifies. [34]Who is he that condemns? Christ Jesus, who died—more than that, who was raised to life—is at the right hand of God and is also interceding for us. [35]Who shall separate us from the love of Christ? Shall trouble or hardship or persecution or famine or nakedness or danger or sword? [36]As it is written:

> *"For your sake we face death all day long;*
> *we are considered as sheep to be slaughtered."*

[37]No, in all these things we are more than conquerors through him who loved us. [38]For I am convinced that neither death nor life, neither angels nor demons, neither the present nor the future, nor any powers, [39]neither height nor depth, nor anything else in all creation, will be able to separate us from the love of God that is in Christ Jesus our Lord.

Romans 8:18–25,31–39, NIV

1. If you had been one of the Christians in Rome and were faced with the possibility of losing your life, your job, your family and friends because of your commitment to Christ, what would be your response to Paul's words?
   ❏ Easy for him to say.
   ❏ Right on—that is just what I needed.
   ❏ I believe all of this, but it doesn't take away how I feel.
   ❏ God, can you make it a little bit easier?

2. Paul compares the suffering of this world to the pain of childbirth (v. 22). How does that affect your attitude toward suffering?
   ❏ It depresses me—childbirth is the most painful thing I could ever imagine.
   ❏ It uplifts me—the pain of childbirth results in new life.
   ❏ It makes me skeptical—I don't see the new life coming.
   ❏ other: _____

3. What is the worst pain you have experienced?
   ❏ childbirth
   ❏ a broken bone
   ❏ passing a kidney stone
   ❏ back pain
   ❏ a root canal
   ❏ severe arthritis
   ❏ psychological pain—a personal loss
   ❏ other: _____

4. When you experience pain, what do you do to make it feel better?
   ❏ grin and bear it
   ❏ just use aspirin, Tylenol, etc.
   ❏ think pleasant thoughts
   ❏ do mind control exercises
   ❏ let everyone know how miserable I am and get them to feel sorry for me
   ❏ Give me some heavy drugs—I'm a wimp.
   ❏ pray
   ❏ other: _____

5. Some Christians teach that if a person has enough faith, he or she will not have to experience pain or grief in this life, because God will spare them from suffering. Given this passage, how do you think Paul would respond to such a view?

> "The Gospels do not explain the Resurrection; the Resurrection explains the Gospels. Belief in the Resurrection is not an appendage to the Christian faith; it is the Christian faith."
> —John S. Whale

6. When are you most likely to say: "Why me, Lord?" Choose three:
   - ❏ when I don't understand what is happening
   - ❏ when no one calls me
   - ❏ when my body aches or I'm ill
   - ❏ when I'm emotionally drained
   - ❏ when nobody understands me
   - ❏ when my boss calls me into his/her office
   - ❏ when it's time to pay the bills
   - ❏ when I'm stuck in traffic
   - ❏ when I'm running late

LEADER: When you have completed the Bible Study, move on to the Caring Time (page 62).

7. How do the assurances of this passage (see especially verses 18 and 21) affect your feelings about the future?
   - ❏ nice thoughts—but I'm still anxious and skeptical
   - ❏ It helps, but I would like to see a little more of what I'm hoping and praying for.
   - ❏ It gives me the peace I need to go on in this world.
   - ❏ other: _____

8. Paul promises that we can be more than conquerors over the troubles that beset us. In light of this promise, how are you doing as we come to the end of this course?
   - ❏ I've raised the white flag.
   - ❏ I'm hanging in there, but I'm surrounded.
   - ❏ I'm starting to "rally the troops," but it's an uphill battle.
   - ❏ I've got the enemy on the run.
   - ❏ Victory is sure and I'm moving into new territory.

COMMENT

Suffering and glory are two concepts Paul wrestles with in Romans 8:18–27. Pain and promise; agony and ecstasy; problems and hope. We are all aware of the stark contrast. Athletes train tirelessly—often at great personal expense—all in hope of winning the big event. Or take Paul's image of childbearing. Although there are few forms of such intense pain, millions of women eagerly bear children each year. It is the hope of children which makes the pain bearable.

But do we know about this suffering/glory pairing Paul discussed in terms of spiritual reality? Are we as motivated by the hope of redemption as we are by the hope of winning a game or bearing a child?

Then Paul leaves behind all the gloom, despair and suffering and captivates his audience with his glorious vision of Christians who are "more than conquerors" (Romans 8:28–39). These words give us hope, no matter what our circumstances or troubles in life might be.

CARING TIME / 15–45 Minutes / All Together

Leader: This is decision time. Bring all the groups back together and evaluate your group experience and decide about the future. Then close in prayer together.

EVALUATION

Take a few minutes to review your experience and reflect. Go around on each point and finish the sentences.

1. What key lessons have you learned about troubles from this Bible study course?

2. As I see it, our purpose and goal as a group was to:

3. We achieved our goal(s):
   ❐ completely   ❐ almost completely
   ❐ somewhat   ❐ We blew it.

4. The high point in this course for me has been:
   ❐ the Scripture exercises
   ❐ the sharing
   ❐ discovering myself
   ❐ belonging to a real community
   ❐ the fun of the fellowship
   ❐ finding new life/purpose for my life

5. One of the most significant things I learned was ...

6. In my opinion, our group functioned:
   ❐ smoothly, and we grew
   ❐ pretty well, but we didn't grow
   ❐ It was tough, but we grew.
   ❐ It was tough, and we didn't grow.

7. The thing I appreciate most about the group as a whole is:

CONTINUATION

Do you want to continue as a group? If so, what do you need to improve? Finish the sentence:

"If I were to suggest one thing we could work on as a group, it would be ..."

MAKE A COVENANT

A covenant is a promise made to each other in the presence of God. Its purpose is to indicate your intention to make yourselves available to one another for the fulfillment of the purposes you share. In a spirit of prayer, work your way through the following sentences, trying to reach an agreement on each statement pertaining to your ongoing life together. Write out your covenant like a contract, stating your purpose, goals and the ground rules for your group.

1. The purpose of our group will be ... (finish the sentence)

2. Our goals will be ...

3. We will meet for _____weeks, after which we will decide if we wish to continue as a group.

4. We will meet from _____ to _____ and we will strive to start on time and end on time.

5. We will meet at _____ (place) or we will rotate from house to house.

6. We will agree to the following ground rules for our group (check):

   ❏ PRIORITY: While you are in the course, you give the group meetings priority.

   ❏ PARTICIPATION: Everyone participates and no one dominates.

   ❏ RESPECT: Everyone is given the right to their own opinion, and all questions are encouraged and respected.

   ❏ CONFIDENTIALITY: Anything that is said in the meeting is never repeated outside the meeting.

   ❏ EMPTY CHAIR: The group stays open to new people at every meeting, as long as they understand the ground rules.

❒ SUPPORT: Permission is given to call upon each other in time of need at any time.

❒ ACCOUNTABILITY: We agree to let the members of the group hold us accountable to the commitments which each of us make in whatever loving ways we decide upon.

CURRICULUM

If you decide to continue as a group for a few more weeks, what are you going to use for study and discipline? There are 15 other studies available at this 201 Series level. 301 Courses, designed for deeper Bible Study with Study Notes, are also available.

For more information about small group resources and possible directions, please contact your small group coordinator or SERENDIPITY at 1-800-525-9563 or visit us at: www.serendipityhouse.com.